GET RICH

REALISTICALLY

Want a 6 Figure Salary and a 10 Hour Work Week?

HERE'S HOW

CHAMPE GRANGER

ISBN: 978-1-54399-643-2 (print)

ISBN: 978-1-54399-644-9 (ebook)

CONTENTS

INTRODUCTION

Are you hoping to win the lottery? Invent an app that goes viral? Inherit millions? Me too. But in case that doesn't work for you, this plan will.

This is *not a get rich quick scheme.* You've heard of those, seen them advertised on TV or maybe bought tickets to some weekend forum promising wealth. Get rich quick is a way to sell you something that results in *the seller* getting wealthy. Winning the lottery is about 1 in 300 million. You are more likely to die getting hit by a bus. You know that. Instead, this is a real plan for real people who want to get rich and know that yeah, it's going to take a bit of work and brain power. But not too much because you have this plan to follow. And because you have me and I've done it *several times.*

Here is your 10-year plan that will allow you to have a career that can make you a 6-figure income annually. By years 3-5 you will only work 20 hours a week. By year 8 you will work about 10 hours a week. And, did I mention, *you don't need a college degree.* And, yes, *you do get to work for yourself.* This book is the true story of my successful battle through the wilderness of business ownership, resulting in a 6-figure income and multi-million net worth. This book is perfect for anyone who wants to *build a great income and even greater lifestyle.*

Inside, I'll tell you *the most important thing you'll do when you start.* You'll learn the things you need to know to decide if you have what it takes to build your own 'RICH'; how to find the right money maker like the ones that made my millions; how to get into it with little or no money for a down-payment; how to push forward when times get tough; and how to sell your efforts when you are ready to make big bucks. Or, keep going if you love it. Right? You're only working 10 hours a week. Why not?

Each chapter starts with some of my favorite quotes from amazing people to inspire us. And just so you *know* that this is not a get rich quick scheme, I'll start by telling you part of the secret right now. *You need to own your own business.* But, you kind of were thinking about that anyway weren't you?

So, let's get started.

FOREWORD

I've been thinking about writing this book for a while. Sadly it took chaos and mayhem in my life to get me to sit down and write it. As you'll read, this was one of my big three (which became big four) goals for the year. But, I could not have completed it without the support of so many people including my family: mom (RIP), GG, Katy, Amy, Jean; other business owners, Myrf and Leah, Bill Sroka, Cele and Lynn, Tara, Margaret, colleagues: Domingo, Andrew S.; family and friends who listen to me and answer my unending business questions or gave me insights: Maverick, Wheeler and Elizabeth, Tom and Linda next door, HLL, Tom Moran, Marcy, Charles, Allison, Stuart Glass (RIP) and the rest of you know who you are. I cannot thank you enough.

WANT TO BE RICH?
NO PROBLEM!

"And will you succeed? Yes! You will indeed!
(99 and ¾%) Guaranteed!

– Dr. Suess

■ ■ ■

Think you're going to invent an app that teaches cats to clean their own litter box? You're going to win the lottery? Your rich aunt will leave you millions? I hope so, but if not, this book provides you with a Plan B (not that Plan B), a plan B for wealth. How will you do it? Selling Tupperware? Wine subscriptions? Vitamins? Probably not. Nothing that sounds like a quick fix often pans out. I bet you've seen someone try those things or tried them yourself. Who hasn't? They all sound good upfront.

How about trying something different? I get it, starting from scratch is hard but following a plan, that's doable. You know, something like Weight Watchers or street signs you can do that. Most of us, reading this type of book anyway, have thought about ways to get rich. Often you've thought about owning your own business. Yes, I let that cat out of the bag. That's part of this strategy but only part of it.

You can definitely run your own biz and, it's not hard if you have a mentor; we all need information and education so let's go through this process together. We are going to identify the opportunity that will work for you and your family. I will tell you how to find it; buy it, maybe with little or no money down; how to run it, get rich and sell it when you are ready. Then, you retire to the Caribbean, the fishing hole or the studio where you've always wanted to learn how to paint. Or, do whatever your dream. By the way, each year this plan gets easier and easier.

Once we have found our business we'll begin to follow this 10-year plan. Years 1 – 3, the beginning, you'll be working hard, 50 – 80 hours a week in order to achieve your 6-figure income. Years 3 – 5 you'll reduce your work hours to 20 – 30 hours a week (not too bad) and still make the big bucks. By years 8 – 10 we will position you to sell your business, get rich and retire if you want to do so. But, maybe you just want to continue raking in the dough? You are only working 10 hours a week at this point. Why not?

Get rich realistically (GRR) in 10 years, it's real start here!

HOW TO GET RICH REALISTICALLY

"Build your dreams, or someone else will
hire you to build theirs."

– Farrah Gray

■ ■ ■

OK so what if I buy into this 10-year plan to get rich realistically? What do I have to do? Beg for money on a street corner? Move to China? Borrow from my in-laws? No, it's much easier than that. There are a number of clear steps, a few years of hard work and then a jaunt down the path of watching and maintaining your wealth until you are ready to sell your business.

As I said before, the primary secret to getting rich is owning a small business. Over 99 percent of America's 28.7 million firms are small businesses. The average small business owner makes $73,000 a year. That's decent, *but you're going to do better.* Our goal is to make 6 figures annually.

A friend once told me that financial advisors seek two types of customers: 1. those who inherit millions and 2. small business owners. Yes, small business owners make big bucks, they build wealth. They invest in their business, themselves and their families and when done, they have something to sell, a bigger better business. Then they get to go to the Bahamas and drink Pina Coladas. That is how it works. But you can't just buy any business and I'll explain that later.

Frankly, it seems like everyone wants to own their own business anyway right? I really can't think of many people that I've met over the years who did not want to own their own business for different reasons. Careers are changing. We are living in the gig economy. Corporations are no longer lifetime experiences. Maybe you want the feeling of creating something? Or you think you can do things better than what's being done out there now. And the answer is, *yes you can.* My recommendations and the plan that follows is that you find your niche and you grow it. It might be a place in several blocks of your home or several miles. But, it will be local and it will be yours and you will do it better.

I'm sure you've heard stories of people who started their own businesses and failed. Sure, we all have. And then there are lots of people who want to own a business, but are unable to take the plunge. Mostly, this is because they don't *understand the risks*, which I will share with you. Once you know the risks and have a plan, you will succeed.

But, what about people, hiring, customers, marketing, money, laws, regulations, social media, unhappy people, cheaters, and nuclear holocaust you ask? I'll cover most of these things and tell you the things that no one else will. Whether you operate a franchise, a single shop or a chain of several you are going to run into these same problems and I'll tell you how to conquer them. The key to solving most of these problems is experience. I learned this the hard way, instead you have me.

In addition, this book will tell you the #1 thing you must do when starting your own business. Yes, there is one very important thing. I will help you decide if business ownership is for you. I'll share everything that is great and not so great about owning a business and help you make the decision to go entrepreneur as I did, if you choose. I'm going to tell you the specific type of business you should own, how to find it and finance the purchase even if you don't have a lot of savings. There are several low cost paths to ownership. Not kidding.

To circle back if you often read articles or watch infomercials or see ads that tell you that getting rich is easy, it's fast and anyone can do it those are *false*. It took Sam Walton 12 years to kick Walmart into full gear. We will do this in 10.

I DID IT SO CAN YOU

"I never dreamed about success. I worked for it."

– Estee Lauder

■ ■ ■

Now we know that owning your own business is the key to getting rich (if you didn't inherit millions). If you did inherit millions, I assume you are buying this book for your niece or nephew that needs a career. Good call. But if this is for you, perhaps you've considered business ownership in the past and think business ownership is just too hard? Maybe you think you need a bunch of money to buy a business? Maybe you fear you won't be good at it? I hear you. When I started, I never imagined myself owning businesses or having done what I've done

LUCK + HARD WORK + SMARTish = Get Rich Realistically (GRR.)

Before the plan, I worked for corporate America for years. I hope you are considering having your own business at a younger age than I was, but if not this plan will work just as well for you as it has for me because it only takes 10 years. I started in technology, which was an advantage to everything I've done since. When I first started thinking about running my own business I remember telling my financial planner "I want to retire at age 50." Well, I didn't really want to retire at age 50 because I would go nuts watching *Dancing with the Stars* and attending museum exhibits for the following 30, 40, years? I didn't want to retire, I just hated my job. And, I didn't really hate my job; I just hated my boss, or the lack of passion that I felt in the company or the opportunities it had to offer. As one of my mentors said 'You want to control your own destiny.' So true, and things are changing, the gig economy, customization, automation, you have to smile and jump from one firm to another to survive and succeed. Feel like a ping pong ball sometimes? No doubt. So did I. One day, I just quit my job on the spot, (I did give them 30 days notice) without even consulting my partner. Don't do that.

I did it because I had already been looking at business ownership and somehow, I knew that I had entrepreneurship in me. My partner had a good job, hallelujah! Besides, during my life I bought and sold some real estate, and felt that sense of excitement of "making my own $$." If you've ever been a babysitter, Uber driver or sold beer at a ball game, you've experienced that feeling too. I knew I could run a business. How? I wasn't really sure, I just felt it. I felt excitement every time that I thought about it. I could envision it. I could see the benefits, shaking hands, hiring, making a difference and building wealth, financial independence and something to last.

I began my journey looking for a business to start or buy. For some reason I was focused on convenience stores. Really? Read on and I will explain why that was not a fit for me. From there I moved to franchises, visiting FASTSIGNS and House Doctors. Unfortunately, my process was not scientific or organized. I attended franchise conventions; I read articles about top franchises and top businesses. I thought about what my community wanted and needed and then decided whether I'd take the next step in evaluating a particular business. But after a year or so, I realized that there were things *I definitely knew I wanted in a business and things that I didn't want.* I've documented a way for you to discover that too.

By the way, you don't need to be an expert in something to run that business. Think math tutoring is going to last but you aren't good in math, that's ok. Believe in auto repair but know nothing about cars, me too. You still might GRR (Get Rich Realistically) doing just that. Do what, you say? (That's my dad's weird phrase 'do what?") Read on, I'll tell you why those will work.

Once I decided what my business would be and purchased it, I worked my fingers to the bone for the first few years, making over $100,000 per year. I grew my wealth and invested in the business and in me. I've loved my work most days. I hate it occasionally and sometimes have the opportunity to gift something to other humans that fills me with pride. I've sold one business making 300% on my investment in one year, not kidding, and I have incredible flexibility in my schedule and work week, if you can call 10 hours a week work. You can have this too.

To repeat, together we will build a 6-figure income for the long term. You'll work less and less each year and at around year 10, you'll be ready to sell your business and hang out on by the lake or move on to the next thing. Or keep rocking it that works too.

I forged this path tripping often. Now, I know better and light the way for you.

HERE IS HOW I STARTED

"Whether you think you can or whether you think you can't, you're right!"

– Henry Ford

■ ■ ■

My business search led me to buy a quick lube. Yes, I'm a woman with a degree in technology. Of, course I bought a quick lube. Did I know anything about cars? Um, not really. Is that OK? Darn right. I knew the basics, but I didn't know the details and I didn't have to.

> **TOP SECRET:** You have one primary job in your business. In terms that we use to describe Queen Elizabeth it's called "smile and wave" and I will tell you why.

We are in an era of making our customers happy. Not just happy but emotionally connected to your business. You need to make them feel important. You need to solve their problems. None of which I knew when I started. What I did know was that the car business, despite the word of the some forecasters was not going away. I personally owned 3 cars for 2 people. Most families I know own 4. Yeah, I get that in big cities people are downsizing or outsourcing or e-sizing their car ownership but all in all we in the good ole'

USA love our cars. Likewise, I knew that cars would continue to be an important part of my community and most of the country.

So while FASTSIGNS seemed interesting and required some technology skills (fit) and I certainly was in need of home repairs like all home owners. I settled on the quick lube. I bought a business that had lots of customers and no profit. Thankfully, I knew why.

IS BUSINESS OWNERSHIP FOR YOU?

"I sell ice in the winter, I sell fire in hell, I am a hustler baby, I sell water to a well."

– Jay Z

■ ■ ■

Did you know that the majority of multi millionaires and billionaires in our country started out in sales? Not surprising. Like Jay Z. they are the type of people who can sell ice in the winter. They look you in the eye and shake your hand and you like them and buy whatever it is they are selling whether you need it or not.

"Yes, I'll take that multi tiered cat scratcher. OK, so I don't have a cat. But, I might be getting one soon."

Recently I hired a guy to cut trees in my yard for $800 even though I already had a bid for $700 just because I liked the second guy. Dumb? Maybe. But thankfully, I've followed this program and already made $$$! And more often than not I spend it wisely.

So, if you are or have been in sales of any kind, you are one step ahead of the rest of us toward success. Whether it was McDonalds or makeup, understanding how to sell makes this plan easier. Sales is not a requirement, as I mentioned, I started out in IT, which has come in very handy. Whether you have a background in finance, marketing, management or being a mom you can succeed with this plan.

Also, *you have to be reasonably financially savvy.* Can you reconcile your check book or checking account app? Do you have a good interest rate on your mortgage? Do you own stocks? Do you have some money in the bank like the minimum of three months expenses that Suze Orman recommends? Do you love to think about how much money you could make if you owned business X, Y or Z? These thoughts do not mean you are a dreamer; entrepreneurs often think about business viability and just happen to think to themselves quite often, 'Wow, there is no one in this restaurant. I wonder how they pay the rent?" or "This place is packed, it must be a gold mine." If that's you, you're off to a great start.

Don't get me wrong. There are people who succeed in business by chance and they are not good with $$$, but they are the exception not the rule. This plan means we are going to succeed; we are going to work really hard for 3-5 years and then work part time thereafter.

Running your biz and only working 10 or 20 hours a week also means you have to:

- Know what you are not good at, *be sane.*

- Be *financially savvy* at home, have savings.

- Be *charming and stable* for at least a few hours each day.

- Be a great problem solver.

To be honest you also need to *know what you are not good at* I think that's one of the toughest things. This is where you need to engage your partner, friends, and mentors. Take your own personal check point on these skills to validate how you might perform as a business owner. It's ok if this plan is not for you *right now.*

Being financially savvy doesn't mean you have to be an accountant, in fact that might be one of the least beneficial backgrounds for entrepreneurs.

Instead, here is an example of the type of financial thinking you'll need: should you buy a new piece of equipment for your business and if so, should you pay cash for it or finance it? OK, well first a piece of equipment = $$$. That tells us we have to determine how much $$$ it will realistically make for you in return. In my business for example I might need to buy a car alignment machine. It costs $3000. I think my customers will need approximately 1 alignment per day. Where do I get that number? I get it from my experience, Googling, talking to people in the business and talking to my mentors.

Next, I need to know how long it will take me to pay off this purchase if I charge $80 per service? In addition to paying for the equipment, I also have to pay my employees to do the car alignment which will cost me approximately $30 per service, so I have to deduct that from the $80. Now I'm at $50 per service profit. Therefore, I will pay off this piece of equipment ($3000 / $50 profit per service) after 60 alignment services. If I think I'm going to do 300 alignments in a year that means profit of $12000 a year on top of which I will then own this piece of equipment which I could also sell if I had to. The machine becomes an asset. So it's a *yes*!

If you skipped over that last paragraph because the numbers were starting to run together and your eyes were glazing over with boredom you might have to work on that (focus) to really crush this entrepreneur thing. Don't get me wrong, I have as much trouble as anyone calculating a tip but what I'm good at is evaluating issues like the one above and what my accountant is good at is monitoring income and expenses at the cents level not necessarily seeing or setting business direction.

However, you can do this; this analysis is no different than what we've all done with respect to Uber or Lyft. Should I get rid of my car all together and just take Uber or Lyft, which means I won't have to pay for gas, car payments or insurance? You know how to do this. You are a problem solver every day. By the way the answer to that question is no. Even my sister who lives in a big city tried to get rid of her car and it became more expensive and inconvenient to rent full time than to own.

Are you charming? You may have heard it before, but people do business with people they like. Right? You are happy to go out to dinner and chat with a friendly bartender and as long as everything is decent, you have a good time. If someone recognizes you at their restaurant, you feel special. If you get a freebie at the car repair shop you might give it a good review.

While the owners of the quick lube I bought did a lot of things wrong, they did the "connecting" part right. The wife was friendly and open with customers. She chatted with them and knew their families. They liked her; so they bought from her, were loyal customers and recommended the business to others (gold star and $$$).

When I say you should be good at sales, I don't mean that you had to have been in sales, you just have to be able to engage your customers. Be a good conversationalist and most importantly a good listener. When I began my businesses I would have told you that I'm not a people person, and I'm kind of not, but I learned to enjoy talking to my customers and finding out about their lives, families, problems and in fact, along the way a few customers I grew to care for dearly passed away. I could never have imagined that would be part of this ride. Over time I would touch customers' lives directly, make their lives better, help their kids with car problems sometimes over the phone and build wealth doing it. Some customers have my managers' cell phone and he will answer it unless he is truly incapacitated or asleep. We care.

Nowadays, we don't often know business owners, especially if a business is not local. Those of us, who own our businesses locally, have an advantage. We can shake hands with our customers and smile we can connect and we have a lot of ways to do that (cell, email, text) that suit our customers.

Of course, business owners *have to be good problem solvers*. That's you if you can multi task, complete a home improvement project, run a family, the PTA or your Meetup group. We are all problem solvers to one degree or another. But in business you are solving problems every day all day long. Ask your friends, family or colleagues, whether this sounds like you. Being a problem solver goes hand in hand with decision making. If you worry about whether you've made the right decision all the time that's probably not best for business because *in business the answer is, there is no right answer* there are good answers and bad answers but unless its math or science, there isn't one right answer. After reading these requirements I suspect you are ready for next steps. After all, these are life skills and you didn't get this far without them.

YOU SHOULD NOT RUN YOUR OWN BUSINESS IF...

"Real integrity is doing the right thing, knowing that nobody's going to know whether you did it or not."

– Oprah Winfrey

■ ■ ■

I can't tell you how many times I've talked to people who say they want their own business. Note that I did not say "want to run" their own business because that's the difference. Running a business is hard work. Following this plan, you are going to work more than full time for the first few years. But, there are other traits that will fail you too. For example:

1. Looking for a get rich quick scheme

2. Dishonesty

3. Being risk averse, overly cautious, have a hard time making decisions, worrier

4. Being a micro manager

5. Being a complete introvert

6. Being a liar, cheat, prejudice or harasser of people

7. You are not able to focus

8. Being super sensitive.

While many of these seem like common sense, there are a few we need to discuss starting with #1 not willing to work hard. It says "willing" intentionally, because we are all "able" to work hard, but may choose not to do so and that is ok. Perhaps that is the right choice for you at the time. One employee told me he wanted to own his own business so he could take his son fishing. Well that's great but he meant like right away, like 3 days a week. That is not going to happen. You can do that, but you won't get rich doing that.

Of course, we are all risk averse to some degree (#4). In fact, Marcus Lemonis, (my hero), from the TV show, *The Profit* on CNBC always says "Being afraid of risk is probably the number 1 thing that keeps people from entrepreneurship." When I left my job in corporate America (don't do that), my partner was earning a good salary and we did not have children. I can't imagine the courage it would take to start a business when you do have a family and all the associated responsibilities. Like I said, in hindsight, I wish I had started my entrepreneurial career sooner because I could be a magnate by now. Although being younger when you go down this path has its tradeoffs. You have fewer responsibilities and less to lose, which is great! Being older you probably have some $$ saved up and perhaps a partner that makes some dough or "hallelujah," has health insurance.

Since this plan means we are going to be hands-off one day, it will be difficult if you tend to be a bit micro-managey? You know who you are. A friend and business owner told me "No one will run your business like you do. " So true. If you are a micro manager (#5) you might still be able to make the big bucks and have the business run exactly as you wish, but *you are going to be exhausted from doing all the work yourself especially for 10 years*. That is not our goal. From that friend I learned to accept "good enough" to provide great service and at the same time have a great lifestyle. Perfect is not the goal.

Several of the above might be intuitive like "you're dishonest" (#3). While there are plenty of rich dishonest people, my feeling is that ultimately you'll be discovered and frankly this program is not for you. The same goes with #7 (a liar, cheat etc…). If any of those things apply to you then you are going to have a hard time keeping staff (see Chapter called Staffing) and again, eventually people will figure you out.

Aren't we all on a 5 second attention span? Yes, me too but successful business owners have to overcome that because focus is critical You will be called upon each day to address dozens of problems and questions and you won't have time to address them all. You'll have to be able to decide which problems or questions get answered that same day, which can be postponed and which won't get answered at all. Yes, there are times when the latter happens to be the right thing to do. You'll hear me repeat this in almost every chapter. *Focus.* Weed out the important from the urgent.

If you don't prioritize the important, you won't' GRR. For example, the people I bought my first business from were great at being car mechanics while the financials failed, marketing was missing, paperwork poor, HR and payroll didn't really exist. I can't tell you how many 'free oil change' coupons I continued to get for years after they were no longer the owners. Focus on your financials before free.

Last, #9 "supersensitive." One of the most important things I'll share with you is that this, *none of this is personal, it's business.* Never forget that fact and instill that understanding in your employees. This phrase will particularly come in handy when you are firing someone.

THE 1 THING YOU SHOULD DO WHILE STARTING YOUR BUSINESS

"Success usually comes to those who are too busy to be looking for it."

– Henry David Thoreau

■ ■ ■

Starting a business is risky. I'm not going to lie. But, you got this. As I've said before if you want to go down this path you should be relatively well-positioned having 3 months savings, a place to live, and transportation and so on. Reminder, 50% of all small businesses fail. So, this is not the plan for you if your life depends on it or you have nothing. If you don't have a job, get one. If you do have a job; keep it, *because the number one thing you should do while you start your business is double-dip.* I did not follow this advice, OK nobody mentioned it either, I just found out the hard way. There are lots of reasons to double dip (keep your day job.) First, if you have healthcare benefits, you are in a great place, fortunate (try buying health insurance as an individual and get back to me). Second, if the business you buy goes belly up, you can return to your career. Third, there may come a time that you decide to leave your job when your business is doing well and that's great but until then, every day has 24 hours; you can work 8 hours for an employer, work 8 hours for you and sleep 8 right? Do that for a year or so.

Before you take the complete plunge you will need a fairly high degree of confidence that your new biz is going to succeed. You might need a year-plus of financials to feel confident that life without the corporate grind and benefits is going to work for you and your family.

Alternatively, if things are not working out (uh oh, are you not following the plan? tsk- tsk) or you just feel like entrepreneurship is not for you, you still have the option of returning to your career. A friend of mine used to work for Comcast. She was a skilled marketing manager. After some years, she and her husband planned for her to leave her job to join him full time as travel writers (he already did that for a living) and follow this type of plan. However, there were times early on when she worried that if she needed to, she would not be able to return to her former career because she'd lost touch with the industry as well as some of the necessary skills. She was right. However, she was also right about leaving because things have gone swimmingly for them both in this full time service biz career and enjoying a great lifestyle.

Speaking of double dipping (or perhaps triple) I know someone who works full time for Google and is a real estate developer. I mean that's two serious jobs. She's smart, hardworking and assumedly successful in both. This comes about from knowing what you are good at and *what you are not good at* as well as having ambition, understanding risk management, having good mentors and a plan.

On the other hand, I've watched one friend go through effort after effort from restaurants to wine club sales to real estate and fail at all of them. I love her dearly, but there is not an enterprise on this earth she could run successfully. So again, for now, keep your day job.

You'll also see this approach (double-dip) used by people who are already rich. They don't just have one source of income, they have several. It might be an actor who sells tequila or a football player who promotes footwear or a model that has a clothing line. This is called multiple streams of income. Not a topic for this book but another form of double dipping.

But, you wouldn't be reading this book if you wanted to work your fingers to the bone forever. Reminder, following this plan, we will work like mad for 3-5 years. Time flies. You'll be able to quit your day job soon enough.

FRANCHISE OR INDEPENDENT BIZ

"I always tell people anyone can get rich, but slow."

– Bill Sroka

■ ■ ■

As I said, when I began my search for a business, I started with a franchises because I didn't have anyone to guide me, as I'm doing for you. I believed that a franchise would provide me with a framework for success, which it can. It also provides you with contacts and colleagues that can answer questions become friends and maybe even buy your business from you (see chapter on Exit Strategy) some day. On the other hand, after about 2-3 years you will continue to pay franchise royalties and not get a lot in return. There are tradeoffs. As someone told me, "they operate the franchise to the knowledge base of the dumbest franchisee which will not be you". So you may get frustrated with progress, change, basics. For example, some franchises may be terrible at marketing, printing flyers in 6 point font front and back with no pictures, explaining the benefits of whatever your service and requiring the franchisees to buy and use that ineffective marketing material.

Or, when the economy is down and the franchise thinks it's a good time to remodel every store at a cost of $25000. You have to follow along or they can sue you. *Yes, sue you.* This may or may not be good for your location.

Don't get me wrong. A franchise does give you a safety net. They want you to succeed because they make $$ from you. You probably thought I would say "They make money if you do." No! They get their money first whether you make money or not. Your franchise can be failing and the franchisor (company that sells you the franchise) can be making the big bucks and drinking margaritas. For example, if your business nets $5000 a month, that's decent. But if your franchise fee is $5000 that means you get zero. Yes, zero. They make $5000 and you get zero. In a win-win situation the goal would be that you net $10,000 and each of you gets $5000. OK, maybe. But be clear. They get their money *before you do*. And, you may end up with nothing.

Franchises are like mini-corporate America. They are going to charge you 3 – 10% of gross income before all of your expenses (not net, which means profit). They will make decisions for you. Good and bad. They should provide marketing and operations, perhaps HR support. Some do a great job of this, some do not. What you are getting is a framework and what you may be giving up is local knowledge, sometimes common sense and sometimes ambition. Keep in mind that franchises will be headquartered somewhere. People who live there may or may not have an appreciation for your market. Perhaps the headquarters are in Dallas, Texas, a great city. But Texans may or may not have any appreciation for the neighborhood or city your biz is in, which could be Seattle or Denver, or Peoria. And, they only have so many resources to spread in order to help with your operations and marketing. It happens.

Think about McDonalds a seemingly well-run franchise. As a franchisee, they may tell you that you have to buy a smoothie machine that costs $5000. OK, that's a lot of money. If you live in Miami or Dallas, you'll totally make that money back and often you can lease the equipment and not pay much up front. But let's say you live in Bangor, Maine. Not sure frozen treats will go over that well or repay your lease cost. All in all McDonalds is pervasive and has the franchise thing down. And, let's be honest their fries rock.

So they might be considered to be like the eldest child, who is successful and becomes a doctor. Thankfully, I've not been a part of a loser franchise (the bratty child) that is borderline dishonest/or incompetent. But, they are out there. Do your homework.

Instead, let's say you decide to buy an independent business and not pay the franchise fee and take responsibility for your own marketing, operations and everything. You might do a great job. Or, you might struggle. The secret to buying an independent business and succeeding is twofold: 1. having a great mentor(s) (preferably in the industry) and 2. joining business association(s). For example, in the car industry there is AOCA (Automotive Oil Change Association). There are a dozen good organizations that will help you work through some of the problems you'll encounter as a business owner and help you GRR (get rich realistically). You could even join your local Chamber of Commerce to find a mentor(s) and coincidentally that might also be a place for you to find your Holy Grail, a business to buy from a retiring owner or a place to someday sell yours. I'll explain the importance of that later.

So the choice is up to you. Give your franchisor on average 7% or do it yourself knowing that you will do some things that are great, cool and appropriate for your market and that you also going to make some mistakes.

WHAT TYPE OF BUSINESS SHOULD I BUY

*"I skate to where the puck is going to be,
not where it has been."*

– Wayne Gretzy, Hockey Star

■ ■ ■

At this point we've decided that we will buy/run a business and that we have the right personality to do so. Perhaps you think you should go with a franchise instead of an independent. Good call if that's right for your family. What should we consider next? Should I sell donuts or day trips? Dog beds or design services? The answer is definitely not a donuts or dog beds. Instead sell a service.

The reason I recommend services as opposed to products is that services are things that typically Amazon and the Chinese or other low cost providers cannot knock off. While, creating a new product is amazing, unless you have $5000 to patent it, if it is patentable in the first place, and you can defend the patent $$$$, it's an uphill battle. I think we often see some product on Shark Tank or an Infomercial and we think "OMG, I thought of that years ago" or "I have like five ideas for amazing products". Yes, you probably do, but the process of bringing that product to market is difficult, not impossible, but difficult. Instead, what I'm sharing are the steps to *get rich realistically*. By choosing the right service, you will have a protected income stream. The way you protect that $$$ is by providing excellent – what's it called? *Service.*

Knowing we are going to buy a service business we need to think about what will work for your family's lifestyle. Why, because you have to continue to live. You have to work in an industry that is going to integrate semi-successfully with your family. Have lots of dogs? You need to be able to afford a dog walker. Lots of kids? You need childcare. Very active in your church on Sundays, maybe you need to make sure your biz is closed that day. In my search I immediately ruled out restaurants and food because I did not want to be working from 7am to midnight 365 days a year. Even though you will have people working for you for the first few years it's you who might have to run that frialator when someone calls in sick or lay those brick or pick up that trash if an employee does not show up. Frankly, I didn't have a background or passion for food. If you do, cool. A restaurant that is run right can be a cash cow (make you a lot of $$$). But, what's the joke? How do you make a small fortune? Start with a large fortune and buy a restaurant. So, think through the times, days and hours to determine if a particular service business is a match for your lifestyle.

What is more, I prefer a business where customers come to you rather than your employees going into customer's locations because staff management and scheduling are simpler. Do you want to sell to retail customers or wholesale? That might be determined by whether you have contacts in a particular field already. Maybe you've been selling cleaning products for years, starting a cleaning business makes sense. Perhaps you are handy, Mr. Handyman franchise might be right for you? Love teaching, how about buying a tutoring firm? These are all good matches and potentially good services.

If you own a business where you go to the customer or into their home, you should have the technology and processes to manage that. For example, you will need to have GPS on your vehicles. Your employees will need to wear booties on their feet to keep the customers site clean and belts so we don't have to see something we don't want to see. Something like a GoPro, the same thing as body cam, is probably a good idea for any employees that enter a customer's home. GoPros can also help from the perspective of diagnosing problems, damage avoidance, training, customer protection, payroll management and building your reputation for honesty. If you are a plumber and pull a sock out of the toilet and decide not to charge you customer for that service you might get some good social media posts about it. Initially, employees may complain about these protections but 1. It's your business do what it right for you and 2. They will likely love them later.

Remember we want to make 6 figures a year. So, we also have to think about how much $$ to put into a business to buy it. Can you grow the business; add hours or days or new services? Will you need to have multiple locations in order to net 6 figures? Perhaps being a tailor or owning a framing shop you might make less than $100k per shop so you may need to have several locations to achieve our goal. Yet, they still should be local-ish and convenient to your other location(s) and/or your home. Reminder, we are all busy, if you have to drive an hour to get to one of your locations, you are more likely to phone it in, ditch it, and not pay attention. My advice is to keep your locations within 10 miles or 30 minutes plus or minus of your home. Technology (cameras, texts, apps) help, but a smile is what sells your services and builds your business.

Because I was good at the quick lube, the franchise often asked me to buy other shops that were in distress. However, those were never convenient and I had the savvy to know that I did not want to drive hours to manage a shop nor did I have contacts in that area. Things have changed and technology makes remote management easier, but there is still nothing like being hands on with customers and crew.

Lots of things to consider but in summary we are going to buy a service business and to help you consider some see below. More importantly, *none of these require a college degree.*

Auto Repair	Child Care	House or Commercial Cleaning
Plumbing	Roofing	Electrical
Landscaping	Property Management	Hair Salon
Massage	Catering	Pet Care
Tours	Entertainment (E.g. Wine and Design, breweries, rock climbing)	Carpentry
Tutoring	Personal Chef	Professional Training[1]

Now that we are aware of some of the types of service businesses that might work for us, let's see how else we might rate our options.

Can the business stand up to the old "Barrier to Entry[2]" test? *Is it easy for someone else to come into your industry and do the same thing at lower cost or better value?* If so, just say no! But, if the business requires expensive tools or machinery, some type of license or ongoing training these are all great barriers to entry, which means it's good to own if you can afford the upfront costs of machinery, licenses, location etc… (these are typically sold as part of the business). For example: general contracting, child care, plumbing, nursing etc… typically require licenses and/or expensive tools or equipment. That means they are good to purchase and might be protected from competition. What type of service does *not* have a good barrier? Nail Salon that's why you see three of them in every shopping center. They are too easy to get into. So don't.

Can you find and afford to hire people to work in the business? Are there trained people in this industry in your area? The answer needs to be "yes"

---

[1] 105 Service Businesses to Start Today, Guen Sublette, 2019

[2] Michael Porter, "Competitive Advantage of Market Leaders," 1979

because we are going to be phasing ourselves out of the business later on. We must have a biz that can be run by our well-trained, incentivized staff. It's great to be a doctor or a lawyer, but if you want to get rich and work few hours in 10 years those are not the careers for you. Those folks have to work 10 hours a day or more, day in and day out. The payoff may be big for them, but this plan is better.

It's important when deciding the type of business you'll provide to consider human nature. Do you look forward to going to the dentist, getting your oil changed or having your shoes re-soled? No, of course not, none of us do. We are busy. People only want to do things that are fast, fun or because they have to or they'll die or be shamed by their friends and family, like colorectal exam or car inspections.

Accordingly the "experience" service domain is really significant today. Perhaps you offer kayaking, ax throwing, dining or spa services, *people want to do these things*. However, in times of recession or depression, people tend to cut back on fun items first. (Recessions arrive every 4 to 5 years (right now is an exception) and last about 11 months on average.) You can definitely succeed in fun experience domains, but while you are raking in the big bucks in good years save your $$$ so we can GRR.

On the other hand, if your service is more mandatory and not fun, dentist, car repair, roof repair etc…you will do OK in bad times and good. Perhaps not rolling in the dough during the bad times, but you'll do well. Your income can be more predictable if you are doing these things. Surprisingly, I had my very best year of sales in 2009, the height of the Great Recession.

I LIKE THIS INDUSTRY, HOW DO I KNOW IF IT'S RIGHT FOR ME

"You only live once, but if you do it right,
once is enough."

– Mae West, entertainer

■ ■ ■

Now, you've decided what type of business might work for your lifestyle and it's a service that meets our other requirements. Perfect. The next step would be to start with a business plan right? No! No one reads a business plan. I don't understand how this is still a thing. Banks don't ask for them, owners don't ask for them, I've never been asked for a business plan in my entire career. The only person that is going to ask for your business plan is a professor or a mentor from a group like the Service Corp of Retired Executives (SCORE). I've written many a business plan and shared none. First, if you have no experience in business no bank is going to lend you money period. You are going to finance your business as I will describe later in the book.

What you will need, for yourself, anyone else who might give you money or your life partner, who may think you are crazy for wanting to start a sand castle building business, is a basic cash flow projection using something like Microsoft Excel or Google Docs.

Specifically, *I recommend you look for a business that you can buy for less than $100k* (maybe more in expensive cities.) 100k! You're thinking where am I going to get that kind of money? Hold your pants on. I'll get to it. I bought one of my businesses for about $80k, the second for $0, the third for $20k and the last one for $80k. On average, if I can do the math without a calculator that's about $45k each. Perfect. Again, sounds like a lot, but we will discuss that shortly.

To achieve our goals, I want you to buy a business for which you will have a 1 to 3 ROI. What's ROI? Look it up! Basically it means when you are going to get your money back and start putting money in the bank in order to GRR. One day your business(es) will gross $1 million or more if run properly. That's our goal in order to achieve a 6 figure income.

If you evaluate the potential businesses cash flow (assuming the changes you might make like opening an extra day, longer hours or new services) and it is not approaching $100k net then wash, rinse and repeat. *Do not move forward* if the numbers don't work. That doesn't mean you can't' revisit your assumptions *realistically*. Maybe you'll have 13 customers a day instead of 10. Maybe you can hire 3 employees instead of 4 in the beginning. Remember, you will be your own employee for the first 3 years remember? You get paid from the profit and maybe not a salary for a short period of time. Again, you have savings, your are sane, and haven't quit your day job. More importantly it's always good to have a savvy friend, mentor, accountant, life partner etc… review the numbers. If you've chosen a franchise, they will provide you with the numbers up front in a document called a Franchise Disclosure Document. Beware; their numbers are always very optimistic so take them with a grain of salt.

BUY A BROKEN BUSINESS

"A pessimist sees the difficulty in every opportunity; an optimist sees the opportunity in every difficulty."

– Winston Churchill, British Prime Minister

◼ ◼ ◼

In order to GRR, I've said that you should buy an existing service business. But, not just any existing business, the secret to my success has been to find a particular kind of business. It has customers, is a good service that will be needed for many years to come, but is being run terribly. I call that *a broken business.*

Do what? Why buy a broken business and more importantly, what is a broken business? If the business meets our criteria (barrier to entry, service, lifestyle, good location, and other people can work for you etc…) *and it is broken*, you'll be able to buy it on sale, and turn it into your own golden egg much like fixing up that bicycle with the flat tire, repainting that distressed dresser, or putting some lipstick on that pig!

"Well, how do I find a broken business? " you ask.

It's easy if you look a bit. Here's why. Demographically, many business owners are aging. In the old days (1970's) people used to retire between ages 60-65 and then sit around and watch the only three TV channels that were available. Now people are living longer and healthier. But from the ages of

55-65 they are thinking about 'retirement' of some sort. So, if they own a business, they may want to sell it. Moreover, some of these business owners, especially if they have been in the biz a long time, get tired and let their businesses decline (the 4th biz I found). It gets dirty, service suffers, they don't mange financials properly etc… *That is a broken business* and it's actually a two-fer because the *owner might be willing to finance the purchase for you.* Home run, a good business, good price and good buy.

You might find such a business as a customer of one of them. When you go there you think to yourself, this place is just not doing it for me anymore and you notice that it's run down.; the owner is never there anymore; things just aren't in good shape. You think to yourself, "I need to find another dry cleaner, hair dresser, barber, painter (or whatever the service)". Hmm, it might be broken and, perhaps perfect for you to purchase.

As I said, after travelling the country, and checking out franchises and deciding I didn't want to own a convenience store or start something from scratch, I bought a quick lube. It met my requirements because it was a service that I knew was going to be needed for years to come It was open reasonable hours and was located only six miles from my house in a growing part of town. The biz had a great customer base; it was just broken. After soul searching and running the numbers, I decided that this was either a gold mine or a death march. Thankfully, it was the former.

Lastly, and most easy to recognize, when your salon starts selling wine and cheese up front, it might be broken. For example, there is an auto repair shop near me that rents RV's. What? Recently I noticed that they had added 'boat repairs' to their sign. Clearly, this auto repair shop is not making enough money with their main gig (principle line of business) and has had to add "crazy" to survive. These are also signs that the business might be broken and again, an opportunity for you to get a great deal.

When I say I bought my second business for $0 that is true. It was completely broken. The owner wanted to sell, but it was a franchise and there were a lot of hoops to jump through that made the sale difficult. The business was failing, no customers. We negotiated briefly with no good outcome. I waited and watched for months until, one day it closed. I contacted the landlord and rented it within a few weeks. All of the car repair equipment was still on-site and some of the employees returned. Since cars only get oil changes two or three times a year, some of the customers were not aware that the shop had even closed. Somehow I got the customer database too. Home run! I ended up redoing some of the cosmetics, upgrading this and that, a few repairs but all in I spent only $20,000, a great deal.

The third business I bought for $25k was broken too. Here's why. The owner of that car repair shop's main business was roofing not car repair. He lived in Florida for half the year and played golf three times a week. All of these facts helped me gather that he was not keen on car repair and wanted out. We began negotiations to buy the business at his price of $80k. Again, I was in no hurry and just waited and, that worked. I finally bought the business for $25k and frankly, we were both happy with the deal. He got out and is successful in his main gig and I got in. Even now, years later we are still each other's customers. Win-Win. Patience is a great negotiation tactic.

> **TOP SECRET:** There are three things in my industry that *imply* that a business is broken: dirty or dated location, lack of technology and lack of marketing. I suspect these three apply across the board. Failed financial management sits atop all of them.

Here's the catch. There may be a reason that the business is broken that you may not be able to fix. For example, no one wants that particular service anymore (like dry cleaning which has declined a bit), Blockbuster video for those old enough to even know what it was or car phone installation (yeah, that was a thing). Perhaps the service can be done anywhere, there is too much competition (accounting, insurance) or the business location has declined. Make sure you think through these issues before buying any broken business.

HOW TO FIND YOUR DEAL

"You can only negotiate if the other person wants something from you. "

– Champe

■ ■ ■

So now you know that *you are looking for an existing service business that is broken* but has good bones, not too much competition, good future and location, all in all a gem. Where do you start to find it? Well, you dig, you get dirty, and you get creative. I bought my first biz from a friend of a friend's tenant. Yeah, hard to understand, but the landlord was not getting paid because the business owner was not succeeding. They had plenty of customers, but had no experience in running a business and starting out *they were not savvy and sane with savings.*

I found my 2nd and 3rd businesses through my vendors, people who sold me supplies and such. In the car biz you buy products from Napa or Advance Auto or O'Reilly's or whomever. Once you've decided on the industry you'll operate in or if you are ready to expand (see Chapter "My Business is Doing Great Should I Expand") ask vendors about other local businesses:

- That are failing,

- That are for sale,

- That have older owners,

- That have owners that live elsewhere or have another job and aren't interested in their biz anymore?

And keep your eyes open. You drive by businesses every day that may be right for you to buy but look awful. You can tell because their signs are broken or faded, their logos are outdated, they don't return phone calls. Yeah, golden goose. Ka-ching! Whenever I saw businesses like that, I asked my vendors, accountant or neighbors about them. I did recon, learning that, yep, that owner doesn't know their head from a hole in the ground or yeah, they are tired, ready to retire or they want out.

I found my 4th business on Craigslist. Instead of hanging on Facebook and Instagram, I tend to look at Craigslist, BizBuySell.com and LoopNet, for businesses or properties to buy. One day I saw an auto repair shop for sale on Craigslist that seemed interesting and I started my research. Location check! Close by? Check! My industry? Check! So I called the business broker who was representing the sale.

I could immediately tell that the owner was kind of desperate to sell the business because the broker said things like "the owner is retiring," "the owner lost his wife," "things are negotiable" and "possibly some owner financing." All of these were signs of a potentially good deal.

Upon visiting the shop, I was delighted to see that it was filthy and that they had a computer that looked something like an old Volkswagen bug that even I with my computer background could not operate. I learned that they hadn't paid for marketing in years because the business operated exclusively by word of mouth. The owner was rarely in the shop but, they had good staff and decent volume. Thus began my negotiation to buy the biz and more importantly, the real estate.

Now you've decided the type of service you want to own. Perhaps a franchise is more in line with your lifestyle and in fact, there might be one right around the corner that is a hot mess. You ran the numbers and they are looking good so, how do you make this happen financially if you don't have tons of dough?

HOW DO I AFFORD TO BUY THE BUSINESS

*" Ask for money get advice.
Ask for advice get $$ twice."*

– Pitbull, artist

■ ■ ■

Well, where in the heck am I going to get $100k to buy a business you ask? If you have read this far, you read the part that says this plan will work if you are relatively financially stable, sane, savvy and preferably have a job. For that matter, it doesn't even have to be a good job!

Let's talk about me. How did I get the money to pay for my first biz? I had $80,000 in cash plus some retirement savings. I was relatively sane, savvy, stable and owned (had a mortgage on) a house. I realize that not everyone has cash and that's ok. Let's say you are a homeowner, you can do a cash-out refi or home equity loan to buy your biz. In fact, that is what my partner for Biz #3 did and what I'm doing right now to buy a piece of real estate.

You can use money from your 401k. This is not preferable because of the penalties and because you will also need $$ when you retire, but it is an option. You saved that money for what's next. Maybe this is what's next? There are also loans from friends and family. I really don't like this one unless *I know for sure* that this biz is going to be a home run. Frankly, I've never done it, although I have been offered $$$ from friends and family because of my record of success. Don't ask friends and family for $$$ unless they are Richie

Rich and the amount matters nothing to them. This is a last resort. You can lose friends and family quickly and things can become unpleasant. In fact, one of my buddies used to tell me, "Don't ever take a partner, unless it's to dance." So true.

But my favorite type of financing is owner financing. If the owner of a business you've identified or perhaps work in already is ready to retire, is not doing well or has other interests, owner financing is a great option for both of you. I used it for my real estate in biz's #1, and #4. You might expect to pay a little higher interest rate than banks are charging and expect to put certain money down. But, you could buy a business that is valued at $100k for just $10k or $20k down payment (typical 20% down-payment) instead of having to pay the entire $100k. Another option is that if an owner has a good employee buyer (you), they might allow the employee to work for their down payment by, for example; gifting the employee 1% of the business each year for 10 years, allowing the employee to build a 10% or more down-payment to buy the business. That means you could buy a $100,000 biz requiring $20k down for only $10,000 because you've earned half of the down-payment via working. I know that $10k and $20k sound like a lot of money and it is but it's much less than buying a new car and you are investing in yourself.

TOP SECRET: Last, if the business property is owned by the business owner also, you are in fat city the true golden goose. But, we'll cover that after we hit our stride in business years 3 to 5.

I also have to tell you about my friend Victoria who owns a dance studio where you send your kids to learn ballet or jazz etc… She owns a business that would probably sell for about $100,000 today and a building that is worth approximately $300,000. She bought both with a $7000 down payment from her retirement. Sure, not exactly because she's paying a mortgage and interest, but that is how much money she put down. She started her business from scratch and did her homework, ran the numbers, knew the location and understood the industry. Ultimately, working with (negotiating hard, proving her worth, being a good citizen) the building owner and the local bank, she got a loan to buy the property. She has a service business that she loves, a building that will be great for her retirement income and only put down $7000 while getting rich realistically. I've heard these stories and lived them myself, time and time again. Not kidding.

THE BEGINNING - LET'S GET THIS PARTY STARTED

"Do or do not, there is no try."

– Yoda.

■ ■ ■

Congratulations! You thought you wanted to be a business owner and now you are. You got this. OK take a couple of deep breaths. It's OK to think 'WTH have I done? Am I going to survive?" Because the answer is, if you've followed the plan, *you are going to survive*. You are not only going to survive, you are going to GRR. You are going to create a successful business, and in 10 years you'll be ready to sell it and retire if you want to do so.

If you've purchased an existing business, which is what I recommended, you will have a turnover or start date and you will have negotiated with the prior owner for at least 90 days support. Make sure the support is on-site, not by phone at least for the first 60 days. Include payments for the owner being on-site or penalties in the contract if they skip out. Hold this money back until the time has expired and he/she has met their commitments. All of which will be written into the purchase contract.

So you show up on day 1 at the open of business wearing proper uniform with logo and looking like an owner, not a sloppy, slacker. First impressions are the most important. Have a short speech planned for your employees telling them how happy you are to be here and own this fabulously successful business and that they are the key to success going forward. This may be a lie. Some employees will have to be fired or maybe they are incompetent and won't be able to fulfill your vision, but it never hurts to say something enthusiastic. You can deal with any dirt in a week or so. On the other hand, *these folks may be the best thing since sliced bread*. Right now, you don't know.

In my opening speech in my first business I talked to my employees about how excited I was to be the new owner. They were excited too because apparently their paychecks had been bouncing for the last few pay periods. I shared my key principles of honesty and a win-win program where everyone makes money highlighting the fact that the owner only succeeds if the employees succeed and we all depend on our customers for that success. I might have mentioned processes and cleanliness because they looked a bit like the *Pirates of the Caribbean*. But, my focus was on mutual success, calming their nerves and generating optimism. Moreover this was a quick lube and I needed them. I wasn't going to be able to do all their jobs myself that was for sure.

In my 4th business we inherited one guy who basically ran the entire business by himself. Bless his heart. He answered phones, did the work and collected the $$$. He had been taken advantage of for many years and was a good employee. We were lucky and, grateful to have him. We quickly changed his role, allowing him to go back to "doing his job" as a mechanic not having to do everything else. Once he figured us out, he loved working for us. He was giddy, happy and relieved. He had been treated poorly for a long time. But his personality was to stay with the business. That's called loyalty which tells you something. He was a keeper.

The first three months in your new world are going to be challenging. I won't lie. You won't know which end is up some days but you'll watch and learn and you are savvy, sane, have savings and you are a good sales person or you wouldn't be here.

For the first three months I had to listen to country music on an AM station. Don't get me wrong, I like country music, but over the course of a 10-hour day you tend to hear the same song over and over again. If you bought a broken business, which you were supposed to do, you won't believe some of the things the employees or the owner (on-site training) for that matter say and do. Sit tight. Listen and learn. Don't try to change everything on day 1 unless it's something awful like cursing, treating customers horribly or dishonesty. We'll learn to make the necessary changes in small chunks soon.

Most importantly, do every task that you can yourself for the first few months. Pick up the mail, send out bills, clean the toilets, talk to the person who delivers the coffee, answer the phones and so on... If you are an outsider, you'll immediately see where improvements can be made. Ask questions. Why do we do this in this way? Why do we have two different companies delivering computer paper? Why don't we use a better quality wiper blade when we have all these defects? Many times the answer will be "because" or "IDK" or "Well that's the way Fred always said we had to do it." Be patient.

One of the most shocking things I experienced during my first week in business #1 was when I asked the manager "Who takes out the trash?"

"You do" he replied with a stare.

I was dumbfounded. Eye-opener. Coming from a job in corporate America I'd never taken out trash. I did say "Thank you" to the people who came in after 6pm when I was still working and handled it. However, I took out the trash at my new business that evening and every day after that I was there until the business sold. It's important that employees know that you wouldn't ask them to do anything that you are not willing to do yourself. That's called leadership.

Your journey has just begun.

RUNNING YOUR BIZ

"The way to get started is to quit talking and begin doing."

– Walt Disney

■ ■ ■

At this point you've purchased an existing broken business and gotten a good price. Perhaps the owner financed it. Yes! Perhaps you know the industry already, even better. No matter, we are on our way to completing the three phases we will work through to *get rich realistically*. As a reminder, in years 1 through 3 (the beginning) you're going to work your fingers to the bone. Years 3 through 7 (the middle) you're going to manage, develop and grow the biz while working 20 hours a week-ish; and years 8 to 10 (the exit) you are going to monitor, improve and plan for your exit. Congratulations. You are on your way to GRR and it works.

Every business, every process has a beginning, middle and an end. Just like thinking about how you're going to exit in 10 years, be rich and do whatever you want that's called the end. When we're excited about owning a business and getting out of the corporate rat race, that is the beginning. The hard part is the middle. If you're like me and you're more strategic and can't stop thinking, the middle can get boring. To keep things interesting and because it's the best way that I know to accomplish goals, we are going to break these years up into continuous challenges daily, monthly and yearly to get you through these middle years.

In today's terms we might talk about Elon Musk the creator of Tesla etc... Genius! Incredible ideas, but, he cannot push through the middle of the operations of his businesses (and there are many). For example, he started Tesla 10 years ago and while that company is progressing it has suffered because he also started three or four other crazy amazing companies during the same time. What if he had not? The middle is why not everyone succeeds; they give up or lose energy or focus. But you will succeed by following this plan. Many people start businesses and many people fail. The middle, operations, running your business, day to day, whatever you want to call it is the hard part. Focus, do this right and you'll be rich. Here's how you keep it going.

HOW I DID THE MIDDLE (YEARS 3 THROUGH 7)

"When you think about quitting, think about why you started."

– Unknown

■ ■ ■

Doing the middle, the hard part, is easy if you break it down into pieces and parts. Every week, every month, every year has goals. It's no different than being on a diet or going to school. Write down your plans, sales and marketing are a must. Write down two or three major business upgrades that you'll do in a year. Perhaps you will renovate your customer waiting area; perhaps you will install a new computer system; perhaps you will install new signs. You can't do everything. Pick three in each category for each timeframe and nail it. Then have a staff meeting every month and make sure everyone is on board.

For example, this year my financial sales goal is $1,000,000. Don't tell anyone but we are going to beat that number. Yes! If you ask anyone on my staff what our sales goal is they will tell you this number without hesitation.

In addition, there should always be something on the agenda to grow and retain your staff. Remember they are going to take over for you and give you your free time. Do something for them every month, perhaps a training class, perhaps a sales goal or a new piece of equipment that will make their jobs easier. Do it. And how do you know what they need or want? Ask them. But it has to help us GRR. Yeah they might say a 50" flat screen in the employee lounge. Thank you, next.

In the next chapters, I've shared my secrets to most every aspects of business including ways you can tackle them in these middle years. Meanwhile, remember, you are getting rich.

STAFFING

"Everyone talks about building a relationship with your customer. I think you build one with your employees first."

– Angela Ahrendts Senior Vice President Apple

■ ■ ■

I'm going to spend a good bit of time discussing employees and related activities in this book because these, them, they are how you are going to work less and less, make more and more $$$ and retire in year 10. Yes, the world is changing; yes millennial behave differently than baby boomers; yes there is a strong gig economy and perhaps in 10 years everything will be gig. More robots will take jobs from people. However, as we stated, we are more protected from that in service businesses it's very much about customer satisfaction, connection and your smile. Robots just aren't there yet, thankfully.

Moreover, the most important thing in years 3 through 10 of running the business is staffing. Prior to that you are going to be on site and meet and greet, connect and serve your customers giving them value. You are going to cross every T and dot every I. But, as the years pass you must be able to trust your staff. Trust but verify. Spot check details, always check customer reviews. When your staff wow's someone, mention it to the employee, or the whole team. A hand shake is old fashioned now days and means more than a text. But no matter what, say 'thank you".

First, know that employees fall into my same favorite context, the "80-20 rule. " 10% superstars, 80% can go either way, and last the10% you should have fired last week. OK that's 80-10-10, but you get the point. In addition, attitude is often everything. I'd rather have a little bit less skilled employee with a good attitude than an expert jerk. Yes, you have to fire people but sometimes you also want to see certain staff move on, move up. They may not be meant for this business but they have great skills for something else. You will see that in them. Don't shoot yourself in the foot letting them go right away, but help them get there.

For example, I briefly had an employee who just graduated from college with a degree in computers science. He was great with our technology, as expected and very good with customers. He knew nothing about cars, but we were desperate. He said the right things about sales. He was on time, willing to learn and thankful to get this job as he was previously working in the cheese department at Wegmans and saw this as a step in the right direction. Eyebrow raise, but good for me. We on-boarded him (that's a hip and trendy 2020 biz term). After a month he was up to speed and really contributing. More importantly he was a cool dude and just pleasant to have as an employee.

Then one day I was informed (he didn't want to tell me himself) that he'd gotten a job offer from a computer company. Darn. Just trained, just hired, and just clicking. I got over it quickly because I could see his potential and knew he deserved a better fit and to work in his chosen career. It didn't make me happy and we had to start the hiring process all over again, but it was the right thing to do, sending him off into the big world of real potential. We still stay in touch.

FINANCIAL MANAGEMENT

■ ■ ■

Just like at home in your personal life in business there are big expenses and there are little expenses. The mortgage, car, food, kids are big. In business it's Cost of Goods Sold (COGS for auto repair are things like brake pads, wiper blades etc…for a plumber it might be a faucet, pipes etc…), payroll and maybe rent. Focus on managing these big costs first. Rent has likely been set (see Chapter 'Rent'.) The rest are dust. Once you are killing it on a regular basis you can tweak the smaller expenses: utilities, accounting fees, marketing, office supplies. Just as you do at home you might refinance your mortgage or move to save on rent (big), but you probably don't shop very hard to save money on postage (little).

Throughout the life of our business, we will continue to listen to what our accountant says, what our cash flow reports say and compare our business to others in our same industry to see if we are on track. Comparing this year's cash flow numbers to last year's is the most helpful because often your sales will be vary significantly month to month. For example, in the car biz we are busiest in the summer when everyone goes on vacation. In the skiing business, just the opposite I suspect.

Assuming that you bought a broken business, we have to fix it. Financial management is often one of the top problems that the business might have had. Business #1 the quick lube cost me $80,000 and returned almost $200k net year 1, I'm not kidding. This was a situation where the mechanic was a great mechanic but didn't have the financial management skills necessary to run a business. And no surprise, because I'm a good business person, you don't want me working on your car.

DON'T TAKE CHECKS

End of chapter.

■ ■ ■

ACCOUNTS RECEIVABLE

■ ■ ■

The most important thing about accounts receivable (money people owe you,) is *not to have them if possible.* However, in many businesses is not possible to avoid them. Mostly you will have accounts receivable (AR) if you are doing business to business (B2B) sales. For example: You own a plumbing company and have 20 trucks with your employees driving around hundreds of miles a day. I own a car repair shop and your trucks need service. You don't want to have to give your credit card to your employees randomly so you set up an account with my business and pay for all the services together monthly.

Or perhaps you own a cake shop and sell a lot of cakes to a nearby caterer. They will pay for the cakes on account at the end of the month-ish. They are not going to send cash over to you or a check for each cake particularly if they buy maybe 10 or more times a month. Too much work.

Accordingly, you will have to bill them via your POS, Quick Books or a similar method. Then, you will have to follow-up because they will forget to pay you, or if they are a struggling business they will avoid paying you. I actually had a guy who ran a carnival pay me $100 in dimes one time. Not kidding. AR are typically thought of in terms of 30, 60 or 90 days due/late. I usually give my customers 30 days to pay without interest. That is generous. Standard terms might be 2%-10, net 30. That means the customer gets 2% discount if they pay within 10 days or 0% discount if they pay within 30 days.

If a customer account is more than 30 days past due start focusing on it. Call them and ask for a specific date upon which you will be paid. Nicely. Ask them for a credit card over the phone. Think creatively. There have been times when I had a customer who was terrible at paying. He was also a caterer so I asked him to cater Thanksgiving dinner for me and gave him credit on his account. Maybe you need something painted and can trade oil changes for that, or car washes, or dog walking. Most small business owners are very open to trade or bartering. It's a win-win.

If the account is in the 60 to 90-day late range, start being more persistent. If it's local, you can drop by. Speak to the owner and always ask for a specific date you will be paid. Start charging interest. Your POS should handle this for you. But, to be honest, if your customer is Whole Foods or Amazon or Target, you may have to be more patient these companies have their own rules and if you want to play their game you have to follow their rules. Another reason we don't want to sell products. They may pay 60 or 90 days or worse. They know they got you. All in all, you have to consider late payments no matter whether they are small or large as a cost of doing business. It takes $$ out of your pocket, so you have to charge more to accommodate that temporary deficit.

Worst case, you may find that you have to take what is called a "write-off" if it becomes obvious to you that the customer is never going to pay. Talk to your accountant if this situation arises and revisit your processes in order to *not* allow that to happen. Successful AR management means 1. Don't take checks (we discussed that) 2. Review and collect accounts receivable no less than bi-weekly and 3. Think creatively.

DUAL CONTROL

■ ■ ■

Is an old time non sexy financial principle that is very valid today and will be until block chain is perfected, which will be 5 years out minimum of this writing. Lucky you, I will update this book regularly. Dual control means that you should never have one person alone responsible for the money. Never, ever. Not even your wife or husband or partner or best friend. If one person counts the money and prepares the bank deposit, someone else will make the physical bank deposit and/or compare it to the POS reports.

The reason I'm saying this is because I had a manager that I loved and trusted with my entire heart steal me blind. He was soft spoken, caring and a church-goer that would impress St. Stephens. When deposits went missing, he looked me in the eye and said, "I put that in the bank last Tuesday for sure." He had a family that I cared for, two little kids and it turns out that he was a bold faced liar. If he had asked me for a loan, I would have gladly given him money and had already signed papers to help him buy cars and rent a house in the past. I don't know what he was thinking .Maybe he truly could not make ends meet and was too proud to ask me again. I knew his mother, his father, his sister, his family. I felt like he was family to me too. Finally when the deposit issue occurred more than once, I called the bank. They really do take video of everything and have access to every transaction by date and time. On the video they could see that he replaced the money a week or so after it should have been deposited. I'm sure he needed it to tide him over. I know he was not buying extravagant items, cars, houses, jewelry he was feeding his family. One thing I've learned is that you truly cannot know what is going on in someone else's mind even though you might think you do. It's business not personal.

It's fine if you have a manager in GRR Phase 2 (the middle) or 3 (the exit) count and deposit money, but then you or your accountant has to verify that the money gets deposited in the bank. And given that most accountants check this only monthly, I'd suggest that you spot check deposits. Every week, check your bank account to see if the exact cash, credit, and checks made it to your bank account in a timely manner, typically 1 – 3 days after they have been received. Tell employees up front that each day, deposits are reconciled with sales and the bank account, and do it. Don't put up with any shenanigans, be on top of it and once an infraction occurs that is the end. There is no infraction #2. This is business. This is math. The money is either in the bank account or it is not. And if it is not that is theft which means that you have to fire someone sadly, simply, sincerely.

POS

■ ■ ■

You might think this stands for piece of shxx but you'd be wrong. It's your "point of sale" device or devices. Back in the day this was known as a cash register. Now we mostly call it a credit card machine. We've all seen Square, used by many small businesses with a tablet or even attached to the service provider's phone. Some of us call it "that swipey thing" but it's a serious issue because 1. this is how you get your $$$ and 2. you need to have controls over your $$$. Your POS *must* provide you with real-time financial reports and key statistics via mobile app. Pay attention to refunds and returns in particular, this is where money can disappear.

Unfortunately, as a business owner, you will have salespeople knocking on your door (literally) to sell you a new POS, all the time. It's annoying, confusing and unnecessary. Here's why. If you operate a franchise, they will make decisions around your point of sale machine for you. Just do what they say. They will negotiate a good rate for you.

However, if you have to choose your own, Square is a great choice. It's not super cheap. As of this writing, you pay 2.75% of sales plus you pay the credit card provider fee (MasterCard, VISA, and Amex) but this is a pretty standard rate.

Your credit card machine will be linked to some kind of software on your computer, tablet or phone that will summarize sales and produce reports for you and your accountant *preferably real time.*

When I began my business, cash and checks were 75% of sales, now they may be 25%. . In fact there are now card only businesses and who knows; by the time this book is published yours might be one of them. But DO make it easy for your customers to pay. Take credit cards over the phone or give your staff that visit peoples homes or offices the "swipey things." Yes there is a risk, but it's worth it. If for some reason you are servicing only 70 year olds, you will have to take cash and checks. That would be unavoidable and it better be worth it.

We know that technology will change and improve. Accordingly, do keep your eye on new technologies that are *faster, better, and cheaper*. But a POS change is a big deal. You have to reprogram your bank account, retrain employees and so on; therefore, don't listen to every offer that comes your way. All in all, the credit card processors have to make a living too and aren't going to process for free, yet! As usual, if their offer sounds too good to be true, it probably is.

CAN I BRING MY PET TO WORK
(ALL DAY EVERY DAY)

■ ■ ■

So, all of the businesses I've purchased have been filthy messes. Granted, they were automotive shops and lend themselves to being less than pristine, but how many times have you been in a hair salon and thought, "What the heck? Do they have their dogs in here?" Or visited a coffee shop with broken chairs and old newspapers lying around. (Is a coffee shop a service? Good question.)

You decide. Do you want to make money or have your dog with you all day? If you say the latter, totally cool, but you aren't taking your business seriously. I love animals. Cats, dogs, birds, fish, you name it, but not everyone loves them. While you may love your pooch, there is nothing worse than dog smell to ditch a sale. Yes, there will be the 10% of people who love your dog as much as you do, 80% don't care and 10% are afraid or disgusted. The Pareto rule, 80-20 rule, remember?

Remember, focus on what you are good at which needs to be sales (smile and wave.) The rest, outsource. If your business is thriving, enjoy your pet at home and hire a dog walker or sitter. Or, in years 3 through 10 walk the dog yourself in your increasing free time. You'll only be working 10 to 20 hours!

RENT

■ ■ ■

Unless you work out of your home, (cool until you have real employees or customers) a big part of the expense of running a business is rent. Where you going to run things? Perhaps it's just some garage owned by a friend of a friend…OK, $1000. But perhaps it's an upscale place in a mall that costs $5000-$10,000. Do what? Yeah, easy and that landlord is going to want you to personally guarantee the rent for the term of the lease. That means, if your biz goes belly up, you will still be responsible for paying the rent. Ouch. Again, refer back to sane, stable and savings. Yes you may be able to sublet the space if that was written in your original contract, but subletting will take time.

Rent terms are also called "Net Rent" or "Triple Net." Triple net rent means you, the renter, pay not only the rent but also the taxes and property maintenance. Triple ouch. Try not to sign this type of lease, although they are very common.

It is possible that you will assume/takeover/re-sign an existing lease held by the person from whom you are buying a broken biz. Never buy a business with less than a 10-year lease unless you know that you are going to move the business and you've already found /own the new location. (Ten years might mean two chunks of 5 years but the annual rent increases must be defined up front.) If you are inheriting a lease, that can be good or bad. In business #3, my lease was crazy cheap $2500/month and it is in a great location! In my first business my rent was expensive $5750/month but, it was affordable because the biz made big bucks. So, don't necessarily freak out over the price, evaluate the risk and reward. Run the numbers.

If you are signing a lease for the first time, the goal will be to get as short of a first term (there will be multiple terms) a lease as possible, to start because you don't know where this carnival ride is going to take you. Ask for 1 year. This seems counter to the last paragraph but what I mean is that get a short lease followed by a 10-year lease, both must be renewable at your discretion. They probably aren't going to give you that, but you can ask and give them reasons. You are more likely to get a short-term starting lease for a property that is empty, or if you don't require the landlord to make building improvements.

Negotiate. If the landlord won't go for 1, go to 3 and then 5 years. Those are the timeframes that realtors/owners will allow. But, require two, 5 year renewals (this is to protect you because your biz is going to be making great money and you'll need those renewals (as I will discuss later.) You will also need a real estate attorney to review the lease. This review is not expensive; it is usually a few hundred bucks. I actually love most real estate attorneys because they are transactional, not confrontational. They get paid by closing the deal unlike other attorneys that get paid to drag out a deal. My apologies to my sister and friends, the attorneys.

Rent is negotiable. All rents are negotiable! If the landlord tells you the rent is *not* negotiable, *it is*. You negotiate by checking rents in the same area or for the same type of business. You can find rentable locations and review rent comps at Loopnet.com. Remember, in business, everything is negotiable. I don't care if you ask your landlord for a free welcome mat. Get something from them.

SERVICES YOU WILL OFFER

'Mostly say no."

– Warren Buffet

■ ■ ■

Every business has multiple products or services (we are doing services.) For example, a nail salon does fingers, toes, regular and fakes nails. A car repair shop does oil changes, tires and inspections and so on. A tour company might do white-water rafting and mountain biking in summer and skiing, snowshoe-ing and spa in winter. Your business will have multiple services too. There are entire books on product development and placement that can instruct you. All I want to say is keep it simple. You can add a new exciting service/product, but at the same time weed out an old dusty money loser. Know which services make you the most money and instead of adding new services, focus on sell-ing the ones that your customers truly want. Check your marketing, does it look awesome, clean, fun, safe, efficient, whatever your goal. Pushing a bad product is no fun for you or your customers.

I've seen many a business adding crappy services that were *hard to sell*. That tells you two things. 1. the customers didn't want the services, and 2. the business model was broken. Remember, we like broken business models except when we own them, ha! Last, remember the 80-20 rule you make 80% of your profits on 20% of your services. Focus on things people really want or need – you might be able to sell cat shoes but it won't be easy. You can easily sell cat sitting. Do that one first.

But, do read, think, talk to your mentors and people in your industry. Always be open to trying new things. And it's OK to fail. It's ok to lose $1000 on offering something new that doesn't work. It's not OK to lose $5,000. So, don't.

THINGS NO ONE ELSE WILL TELL YOU

"Complexity is the enemy."

– Louis Guttierez

■ ■ ■

When you think about owning your own business you see freedom. You envision welcoming your friends to your spa, shop, garage or brewery; laughing, patting each other on the back and them saying to you "Oh wow, this is awesome. You must be loving this." You envision vacations, taking off sunny afternoons and going on school trips with your kids whenever you want, and you will. But, first you have to *dodge the dreadful.*

The dreadful are things that nobody ever mentions when they discuss their business even though their business may be very successful. Now that you know you can run a business, I'm giving you a chapter on the drudge that no one else tells you about so that you have a reference when the time comes. And, it will.

Taxes and fees. This is not a political statement. No one likes taxes; we know we have to pay them. However, there are crazy fees for things that you will never understand. For example, I've been paying a $10 litter tax every year. The billing for which costs me and the city more than $10, I promise you. There are city, state, federal, product taxes, litter taxes, inspections, building inspections, fire extinguisher inspections, tire taxes and others you've never imagined. Each industry has its own and it's not just the cost of the tax, but the administration. Don't forget to account for these items when you project your cash flow *before* you buy the business. Be a good bookkeeper or hire one so that these things do not distract you. Yes, you can pay them all online, but each has a separate login ID and password, and you will only use most sites once a year so you'll forget your password and have to start all over again (awful).

Occupational Safety and Health Administration (OSHA) – take one of these classes. They only last a day or two and are actually interesting. I always send one or more staff each year to one of these classes. The certificates look good on your office wall if OSHA visits. You can find these classes affordably at Pryor.com, careertrack.com and other websites that also have other good classes about things like financial management, sales skills and so on….

Tools and equipment. You need to think of these things as very disposable or *depreciable* (same thing biz term). Some employees will not use your tools and equipment with care. In some industries, salon, auto repair, Uber employees bring their own tools. That is an enormous plus. Whatever you do provide will disappear, break, or wear out regularly so plan to replace these things often. It's called "the cost of doing business." And again, dial that into your original cash flow analysis. If you don't know how much things cost, just use a percent like .05% of gross.

Insurance. Business insurance is much more complicated, painful and more expensive than home or automobile. For example, my home and auto run $3000 and my business insurance runs $12,000. However, my business is full of devastating risks like tires and wrenches heaven forbid you have scissors in your biz. Definitely don't check 'yes' on the box that says 'Do you run with them?"

You are going to get sick. This sounds weird but when you start your business you are going to come in contact with new people, places and things. I used to work in corporate America and then suddenly started interacting with the general public and cash $$$ (ewww). I hadn't been sick in 5 years or more. But, I got very sick perhaps three times my first year of business. However, because I was in year one, I had to work through the illness. One time I had to go behind a fence and lie down on the grass. Not glamorous or professional. It's like when you send your kids to school for the first time and they start eating new germs. So, wash your hands, as usual, but forewarned is forearmed.

FRICTION

■ ■ ■

Friction in business means stuff that is not helping anything and takes away from you making $$$. Reminder, that's what this is all about, GRR. Let's say the brakes are stuck on your bicycle. Even though you're might be peddling hard, the bike isn't moving forward as fast as it should. That's friction. Or, you can never find the clicker also known as the "remote control" for your TV so you search only to find it in the bathroom and you do this same thing the next day too. These things are activities that add no value. The same thing happens in business.

Here's how to deal with friction. First, notice it. That is sometimes hard to do because you are so in the business moment focused on connecting with your customers. In addition, you often don't notice it because it might start small and grow, much like our stomachs. One way that I try to identify friction is by asking new employees what they are seeing in our business that could be done better or differently. They come in with a fresh perspective. I also ask friends or colleagues to come and walk through my business and am *very* open to their feedback. You have to be. Remember, this is business it's not personal.

They might say something simple like 'why does Fred have to walk all the way over to the corner of the building to pick up the wrench that he uses so often?"

And, I will answer "Wow, I don't know. We've just been doing that all along". Then, I change it, and move the tool closer to Fred's workspace eliminating the friction.

Here's a tip. If the same problem has occurred several times in your business then it's causing friction. For example, it makes me crazy when my employees tell me there is a problem with the printer. Because of my computer background, I'm still the shop IT guy.

I will ask, "What's going on with it?"

And they reply "Well, it skips pages and has been doing that for a number of (weeks, months etc...)"

Well, that's helpful to know, I think to myself. "Why didn't anyone tell me this?" I ask with steam coming out of my ears.

To which employees will disperse and pretend to go back to work or say "I told so and so about it." Well, "so and so" left a month ago or is off today.

If your employees tell you once a week that the printer jams or is broken. It's time to buy a new printer or dig into the issue and find out what's causing the problem *and fix it*. Take a moment, run some tests, the problem might be something as simple as paper humidity (common in car repair because garages are not climate controlled). If the problem is too big, stop. You don't do printing for your business that's not what's making you money so that printer and the complaints are friction taking away from the things that you need to do to GRR, get rich realistically. You might need to hire a technician.

We all get busy, trapped, can't see the forest for the trees, especially in years 3 through 7/8. Do something once a month to streamline, identify, and remove friction. Buy your buddy/ gal pal a beverage and walk the shop, making it a two-fer.

THE MIDDLE, CONTINUOUS IMPROVEMENT

"Getting better all the time"

– Fryer et al[3]

Continuous improvement is one of my greatest secrets to success. Actually it's not a secret and it's not mine, but it is how I run my businesses and frankly my life. It especially helps you push forward during the middle years. Each month set one significant goal for improvement at least one, and no more than 3. Focus on those, get them done and do that again the next month. Set three big goals for the year. One of those will be your sales goal. Another might be a renovation, hiring a new manager, acquiring a big new customer or starting a new service.

I failed at this for many years. I tried to do everything possible to make my businesses a success all of the time. Sounds like the right thing to do right? While my businesses were successful, this approach caused me to be stressed, impatient and sometimes not fun.

Now, I set (and you should as well), one to three little goals each month and three big goals each year. Share these goals with your employees, set financial rewards related to the goals and celebrate when they are achieved.

---

[3] Fryer, Karen J.; Antony, Jiju; Douglas, Alex (2007). "Critical success factors of continuous improvement in the public sector: A literature review and some key findings" (PDF).

If you don't achieve a goal, reflect and talk to your mentors and employees to understand why you didn't meet the goal. No excuses. Tweak it maybe and get back on that horse and keep moving through years 3 through 7 because you know at this point you are only working 20 hours a week. Congratulations.

PRICING

"A sale is when the price of something gets so low you finally realize you need it."

– Stuart Glass/fortune cookie

■ ■ ■

So, pricing is a guessing game, but I learned much of what I know from a book[4] called "*The Discipline of Market Leaders,*" an easy read, a beach read in fact in which they spell out the three pricing strategies that you need to know. I have added two more in this section, which are particularly important today.

In this book the authors talk about 3 types of pricing based on:

1. The best product in the market, (iPhone)

2. The best service in the market and (my car repair shop)

3. The cheapest product in the market (Walmart).

They describe each of these in easy to understand detail, most of which is still relevant. Suffice it to say, you will need to decide which of these you are, yes, you can be a bit of a hybrid, but no, you cannot be 50-50 or even 33-33-33. You will have a primary pricing strategy for your business determined by who your customers are. If your customer base is wealthier offer the best

---

[4] Michael Treacy and Fred Wiersema, The Discipline of Market Leader: Choose Your Customers, Narrow Your Focus, Dominate Your Market (1997)

product or service, less affluent market offer great service, if your customer base is poorer perhaps offer services with a lower price. Again, we are talking about services here not products. You are going to match your pricing not only to your customers wants but also to their pocketbooks.

For example: Two carwashes, one located in Richville and one is located in Poorville. The carwash in Richville charges $20 a wash and the carwash in Poorville charges $10 a wash. The primary expenses are cost of goods (which could be equal in these two scenarios) and personnel. Well, the Poorville wash has either nobody (might be self serve) or one person on staff. The Richville wash has three people on staff at all times because those customers expect a higher level of service for the higher price. The rent in Richville is a lot more expensive too. Bottom line, both owners can make the same amount of money if they price their service properly. One chooses to be the low-cost leader and the other, the best service. Both make $5.00 per wash and do 2500 (25 business days x 10 washes per day) washes a month = $12,500 profit per month which equals $150,000 net per year. This is how we do it!

While I don't recommend locating in the poorest of demographic areas, you can make good money with lower to middle income customers. My first shop grossed $1,000,000 where the median income was $55,000 (solid middle income).

My add: Subscription Services

Subscription services are the holy-grail that in business, we are all seeking. Having money pouring in monthly hopefully charged to a credit card and at a price that the customer doesn't even care about unless they are really strapped. Under $20 - $50. So, the carwash example again, $19.99/month or whatever is appropriate given your location / pricing model. If your business can supports a subscription service and you aren't offering it you are losing big bucks. In fact, I know a car wash owner who does not. They are missing out substantially. The owner told me, "It's just too complicated, people wanted refunds, the machine didn't work and so on." I wanted to say "Listen lady, you make that machine work because it's spitting out $20 bills and you need to catch them in a big Hefty trash bag and put them in the bank".

Think Netflix, think health insurance (ouch), think car payment, think Massage Envy. Please, start your own subscription service and rake in the big bucks. Why don't pizza companies do that? A monthly subscription and you get your family's favorite pizza every Friday night, high five, done!

My pet peeve is companies that have amazing subscription opportunities, but never sell them or follow-up. For example electricians, plumbers, roofers etc… Yes, some of them will sell you a protection plan that they might pocket and hope you will never call. But if they were smarter they would go to your home or business and do a biannual inspection and sell you the stuff you truly do need. Maybe they throw in a freebee every year or every visit or better yet, they just call and tell you what you need over the phone based on the age of your home and systems. They schedule an appointment with a two-hour window (hopefully); they show up, get the service done and have one of those little swipey things on their phones so I can pay by card. That's called service! Don't forget, people are busy they have problems; your job is to solve them.

TOP SECRET: Subscriptions are the world's best pricing model.

My Other Add: Convenience

We all understand convenience, it's 7-Eleven. When you offer convenience, unless you are Amazon, you charge more. What if I offer you a free loaner car when you drop your car off for repair? That is convenience. What if I pick up your expensive rug for cleaning and return it to your house on the floor and roll it out nicely exactly where you want it – convenience. What if I come to your home to sign documents instead of you coming to my office – it's a convenience. You automatically charge a premium. This is closely associated to "best service" but I think there is a distinction now between coming to the customer, "the last mile" (very 2020!) versus fantastic service *at the business site.*

TOP SECRET: No matter what pricing philosophy you choose, there are always going to be people who think that your price is too high.

I dealt with this all the time and it's humiliating the first few times around. In my early days when someone complained about price I was like "What?" or "I'm sorry, you're right," or what I wanted to say was "Out of here you jerk" these are all bad responses. As a business owner, you need to have a message that allows your customers to accept your pricing, whatever it is, and relate it to your pricing model. So, if you are charging a fortune and getting a fortune, you say 'I cannot thank you enough for your business, I understand your concern, brilliant, here is a free container of caviar." If you are providing the best product in the world you say "But people like you, know that this is the very best product and by purchasing it the world sees that you are well-informed." If you are providing the least expensive product you say 'OMG so sorry, here's a free bumper sticker, pack of gum, sample shampoo or car air freshener" something cheap.

In business, everything comes back to this formula: Number of Services x Price- Costs=Profit.

Assuming you are running the business according to this plan, if you charge a high price, you don't have to sell so many services (for example a realtor who gets $10,0000 on a sale) might sell 10 homes a year. Excellent. However, if you charge a low price you have to do a lot of services; for example, dry cleaning at $10 per takes 1000 pants to make $10,000.

I know that some of this is common sense, but when you start running your business you need touchstones. Even I have to go back and remind myself. OK, not everyone is my customer. My customers are seeking convenience. Remind yourself that you have a pricing model and stick to it. But do revisit it every year and make sure that it still makes sense. Know that it can change particularly as/if your customer base changes.

EMPLOYEES: THE GOOD, THE BAD AND THE UGLY

"Working just enough to not get fired."

– Meme.

■ ■ ■

If you have children, you will have the upper hand when managing employees. You will see the same shenanigans your kids play. They know the answer to problems or they know how to find the answer they will just come to you and ask because it's easier or they want attention. If you know that they know the answer or you know that you've trained them properly and they know how to find it, simply ask "What do you recommend?" It's much like you might hear at home "Where's my lunch? Where's the TV clicker? Where's my swim suit?" These conversations will suck the life out of you if you don't turn them around and send them off to find the answers on their own. Once they know that you are always going to turn the conversation back to them they will stop asking and start solving problems themselves.

If you've managed employees before, or been an employee you know that employees can be quite challenging. If our business didn't have employees, anyone could run a service business. However, employees also make you money and allow you to transition from working exhaustively to Phase 2 (the middle), working 20 hours a week. And even better, phase 3 during which time these folks take over and allow you to work 10 hours a week while you GRR. Seriously.

Going from corporate employees to blue collar employees, I didn't know what to expect. I was very positively surprised that frankly people's work ethic was the same. Some are good, some are great and some are awful. The biggest difference is probably in the realm of appearance and professionalism. For some reason a number of my employees don't seem to realize when they are using foul language. Don't get me wrong, I've used it on occasion myself, but not at work. So a prohibition on foul language goes in the employee handbook.

Or if you aren't from the same background as your employees, working with new folks might enlighten you. After a few months at the quick lube, I was kind of getting the hang of things. During downtime (yes, you have downtime in your business) the staff and I were stocking inventory. Cool. I was chatting with one of my techs and mentioned something like "I like to take a Laissez Faire (come what may) approach to x." I can't even remember the subject. And he said, "Really, where's that?" It took me a few seconds to understand that he was asking where that fair (like a carnival) was being held. And, I relished that moment, because it was a learning opportunity for me. I recognized my life had changed dramatically. I needed to learn a different language and to fit in. You will have these moments too as you move up or down the socio economic chain or to a new industry. Lesson learned it may require personal change in order to relate to your employees and customers and thereby succeed. But it's worth it because you'll be rich.

Try not to tell your employees how to do things. Teach them what you want done and to "make good decisions.[5]" If you have kids, you are probably already good at this. Set goals for them. Tell them your business principles, which first should be honesty.

Safety is a very big one these days too, although it's gotten a little out of control. "Yes Mildred, I know we are stamp collectors, but according to OSHA, our profession requires safety goggles and mechanics gloves." Or this type of safety requirement: "All of you who work from home must now take the following 1-day course called "Freshly Brewed Coffee Is Hot, Even at Home."

---

[5] Marcy LeSieur, Mom Extraordinaire.

Granted, it will cost the business $250 per person in lost wages, but it saves us $25,000 in legal fees and damages. My recommendation is that if someone does not know that freshly brewed coffee is hot then you should not hire them. And, if you incorporate coffee temperatures as a standard interview question, then in theory they cannot sue you.

Don't get me wrong if you are running a sloppy biz and someone slips and falls and truly hurts themselves in your business, it's on you. Report it, fix the problem and don't let it happen again. However, you will find that just like with customers there are both honest and dishonest employees. Sadly, you have to keep your antenna up and be aware of those who are dishonest, knowing that this is not your primary job. Your job is still sales. So, clearly, "you're going to be busy". But it gets easier as time goes by.

One of your biggest challenges will be managing your employees. Whether you have 2 or 20, whether you have men, women, tall, short or of any nationality it doesn't matter. These are the people that will allow you to make 6 figures and get rich. Perhaps you have to look at them with $ signs on their forehead to get through the day. Do it. But I will also say that some of my most meaningful, memorable and learning moments in this journey have been one on one with my employees.

HIRING

'You are always hiring."

– Champe

■ ■ ■

What's important in selecting employees is that they reflect your customer base. Diversity may be one way to say it or simply the right person for the right job. One of my mentors called this 'Aces in their Places'. If your customer base is 50% black you need to hire some black people. Not people just because they are black, but qualified, capable black people. If your customer base is 50% women, you ought to have a woman in the biz who might relate better to those customers. Remember, we talked about connecting with our customers. Obviously, my field, the automotive industry has very few women employees. Although women make more than 50% of the purchase decisions related to automobiles and most any purchases for that matter, yet often lucky for me; shops are almost exclusively staffed by men. Does that facilitate the connection we are seeking? Probably not.

Unfortunately, no matter what you think, one of your employees is going to quit, leave, get married, move, or go back to school, whatever. Life happens. As long as they do these things in a professional manner you should celebrate their departure. Recently, a friend told me "You know you don't need to give two-week's notice anymore, that's not really a thing." Wrong. Wait until you own a business and then get back to me. I'm always happy for an employee that is moving to a better job, going back to school or trying to improve themselves.

If I can't offer opportunity, I should send them on their way with a smile. When I sold a business recently, I was very sad to lose 10 employees with that deal. However, I've kept in touch with most of them and let them know that I care and am here to help them grow in their careers and life. You also never know when you might want to hire a former employee as long as they are go-getters, keep things positive. The first time I went back to see my former employees I handed each one a $50 bill. I want them to know that I still care.

Connecting with employees is as critical as connecting with your customers and that might require that you change. For example, I am a very task-oriented person I like to get things done. The minute I enter my business I'm scanning for *"to-dos"*. Those things my employees should have done but have not. Clean the bathroom, file paperwork, change signage, tidy their workspace, fill up their company car with gas, etc... I had to change my behavior to be more people oriented and come into my business with a smile and greet each employee, say hello, ask them about their weekend, their husbands, wives, children and their teams. Now, I truly, I enjoy that conversation. But it's not natural for me. So, just be aware of your personality. In service industries, today, people continue to be the most important asset. Don't forget that or these things:

- Offer a referral bonus to your employees who recommend a friend that you hire,

- Recommended hiring sources: Craigslist.com, Indeed.com,

- If you have to fire people, follow a defined process and document it;

- No surprises. We don't like surprises in our business and our employees don't either;

- Set direction, visions, and goals for them, make sure they get it;

- In years 3-5 identify potential leaders and pay special attention to their development;

In years 8 through 10 your leaders should to be able to run the business without you. You want them to be able to *text you the daily stats* or issues (hopefully you get the numbers on your biz app instead) so that you can tell whether you've had a profitable business day or not. You'll know which stats are important in your first three months of business.

This may be obvious, but your payroll, scheduling, benefits etc…has to be fully automated. Some of my favorite payroll orgs are DominionPayroll. com, SurePayroll.com. and for scheduling: WhenIWork.com

Don't micro-manage. I told you early on that this is a no-no. If you are micro managing employees you aren't selling. Your job is to smile and sell.

Give employees the tools they need to do their jobs but make them accountable for those tools. This might mean something as easy as assigning a tool kit to them, document tools and require employees to turn them in if they depart the business. Put it in writing. Charge them a fee if the property is not returned (in line with state and federal HR laws).

And then there are the employees that hold you hostage. This is an employee that you think you cannot live without. You think they make you all your money or they open and close the shop and always show up, which they might. You've tried hiring their replacement, with no success. Or it could be the employee who insists that everything be done their way, argues constantly, refuses to hear options, won't change and basically makes everyone else miserable. Well, I'm here to tell you that *everyone is replaceable.* I've had at least four of these characters on staff in my businesses and sweated over each one. But the minute I fired them or they quit, it was an enormous relief. I did a dance. Whether I had to work hands on every day or pound the pavement to find a replacement or make less money for a short period of time it was worth it. Fire them following proper process. Think through it, again you are sane, stable and savvy, but no one person can be allowed to make anyone in the workplace unhappy or uncomfortable. You will thank me.

My latest hostage-taker did make me a lot of money, but he truly made the other employees miserable. They dreaded coming to work each day. He cussed like a sailor, told people off, played music at deafening levels and everything was his way or the highway. At our first team meeting after firing him, everyone was relieved and at ease. While you should not discuss hiring's and firings, in small teams, you have to acknowledge the "loss". Moreover, I had to apologize to my staff for not firing this guy sooner. He was unbearable and made their lives miserable. That's not OK. I'm the leader and it's my job to create a healthy working environment. Since his "loss", we've had great, fun team meetings, changed the music, eliminated most of the foul language and hired his replacement. Wish I'd done it sooner. Not surprisingly, a month after getting fired he called and asked if we would reconsider and take him back. Yeah, that happens all the time, both with employees I've fired and employees who have resigned or quit. I pay my employees well and treat them well. Sometimes they have to go elsewhere to realize that fact.

And when they go, it's called turnover. In any business you will have employee turnover and here's how it works. 10% of your employees will stay with you through thick and thin, to the death and beyond. 10% of your employees will quit before or soon after they arrive, we call this the revolving door and the other 80% (80-20 rule) will stick around more or less. I'm sure you understand the value of that rule by now. When they leave, you have to hire new employees, but since you are "Always hiring," you might have someone already in mind.

TOP SECRET: When I say "find employees," I mean that. While you can use Craigslist or Indeed, I often actually "find" my employees.

We are all out and about, meeting people day in and day out, from the garbage man or woman to the nurse practitioner at your doctor's office. Wherever you go, always be on the lookout (BOLO) for people who are bright, enthusiastic and offer great customer service.

Shopping in the Dollar Tree one day, I was five deep in line, arms full, foot tapping, trying to decide whether or not I would just dump it all and run when I saw an employee running around the cash register area saying "I'll be right with you guys. Sorry for the wait". This how I met Donnie. He quickly cashed out the four people in front of me and handled my pile with a smile. I slipped him my business card and said, "You're great. I'm hiring. Please come by and talk". He did. We hired him. Not only did he make more money with me, he has a job that is more of a career and I love that. You never know where you will find your next employee. Keep your eyes and your mind open. Just because someone is a dishwasher doesn't mean they can't become an electrician's assistant. I'll say it again, you are always hiring.

CUSTOMERS THE GOOD, THE BAD AND THE UGLY

"Even if you are on the right track, you'll get run over if you just sit there"

– Will Rodgers

■ ■ ■

Again this assessment has an auto repair slant, but you'll get the sense of the challenges you will encounter when dealing with customers. For example:

- Yelp Review: 1 Star "You told me my car would be ready in a few hours and instead it was ready in 1 hour. That is poor communication."

- "Hi Mr. Jones, we've diagnosed the problem with your car not starting. Sir, just wanted to let you know that it's out of gas."

- "My car makes a revving sound whenever I push on the gas. Is there something you can do about that?" Sorry, no. It does that.

One of the jokes you will hear among business owners is that if you didn't have to have employees or customers, running a business would be easy. And, that is true. But that is not in this book "Get Rich Realistically." It might be in the book, "Get Rich Quick" or "How to Scam people." That's not us. You need customers, they pay the bills, most of them are wonderful and they will allow you to retire realistically in 10 years.

The keys to cultivating customers correctly are:

1. Identify your customer base and always keep them in mind.

2. Give your customers more than they expect.

3. Gracefully fire people who are not your customers.

4. Assertively fire customers who treat your employees badly.

5. Smile and wave, be present, connect.

We talked in previous chapters about identifying your customers. This is still a must and you have to write down and constantly refer to the statement defining your customer base. It will look something like this:

- Mom aged 25 – 45 with income of $50k and above

- Men who like to vacation solo with income of $100k and above

- Family with kids with income of $100k and above and live within 5 hours of my business location.

You want to capture the right demographics, male/female, age, income, kids etc…Write these on your bathroom mirror, your hand, the wallpaper on your cell phone, wherever. It's easy to forget the definition of who your customers are and instead to begin chasing cats (instead of your customers).

TOP SECRET: You can find customer demographics for FREE at USPS.com. Look at the Every Door Direct Mail page at postal routes. You can see great demographics showing number of residents and businesses, age and incomes. This mailing service is quite decent too.

When a person comes in who does not fit within your customer base you may never make them happy. Higher income people might pay any amount of money for your service but require perfection that may not be your goal. More price sensitive people might accept a lower level of quality or service, but beat you up on price. An expert in bicycling might not appreciate your bike rental service if the bikes are standard. While you shake hands and appreciate your customers, know that it is OK to fire some of them. You don't want them to be incessantly unhappy or you/your staff beaten up no matter how hard you work. Not everyone is your customer.

By years 3 through 8 you will learn who your best customers are and what they want. This may change over time. Do they want a discount? Do they want perfection? Do they want easy in, easy out? These concepts relate back to "*The Discipline of Market Leaders*" (cheapest, best service, best product). Although to be really successful and work less in years 3 – 5 you need to document your customer's preferences in your POS (point of sale) system, identify the their preferences including details like dog name, birthday and so forth to inform employees about each customer and help employees sell service offerings more effectively. For example if your business cleans rugs you might want to up sell or add-on some type of freshening scent for people with pets. If you run a cake shop definitely send out a birthday coupon.

One of the biggest challenges in managing your business is dealing with unhappy customers. How many unhappy customers are you going to have? Well, if you are doing well, you will have 3% or fewer unhappy customers. It's a small number. If you have 500 customers a week most likely there will be about *15 a week that will be unhappy*. But, if you have 10 customers a week, you should only have *7 or 8 customers a month that are unhappy*. The majority of your customers will be satisfied with your service and an equally small number of people (3% or so) will be ecstatic. Compliments are delightful, money coming in with no drama is great. But, if you are like me in my early days, you'll take *complaints* very personally. Don't!

Remember, this is business it's not personal. If someone is unhappy with your service the reasons typically are:

1. They are just having a bad day.

2. They just are not living their best life.

3. You messed up.

4. You didn't mess up but it's cheaper or easier to make them happy than to argue.

Occasionally a customer will return or reach out and tell you they are having a problem after the service. My friend Paul taught me a simple phrase that helped me and my staff deal with irate customers and it is "LAST".

LAST acronym for:

1. Listen to the issue.

2. Ask questions.

3. Solve the problem.

4. Thank the customer.

Corny perhaps? Effective? Absolutely.

The most common problem in any business of any size is miscommunication. I've worked at the largest and smallest of firms and this always rings true. The answer to miscommunication is to identify where it took place and to correct the problem for the future. Perhaps the miscommunication was on the customer's side, if so; graciously point that out and more often than not the customer will apologize and thank you. If it was on your side, apologize and correct the problem within your organization and follow up to make sure your processes have changed.

If the customer is not being reasonable (i.e., it was their fault and they won't drop it or work with you) say things like "I'm sorry you had that experience" or "I hear you". You are not admitting fault, just listening to them which typically is what they (or anyone) want, right?

If they persist, give them something free or a credit. *$100 Store credit only costs you $50 in most businesses.* Always offer credit first rather than a refund. If they are not a good customer (you don't make money and/or you've never seen them before and they are screaming), say "I'm very sorry. I don't think we are going to be able to make you happy as our customer. I wish you the best." Walk away. This situation will not get better. In my business we document that information in our computer system by adding *"DNR"* (*do not resuscitate*) after the customers last name. I would only recommend doing this for people who really have worn you out on several different visits. Not everyone is your customer.

The worst customer I ever had was a young woman that came to my shop for an oil change.

As she was leaving she came back in and said, "Hey, you guys broke my radio. I want my money back" I didn't mention that an oil change does not relate to the car radio. Instead I said 'OK, no worries, we will check it out."

Unfortunately, that person was already having a bad day *and* they were not living their best life so it became the perfect storm. Although we immediately ran out to check out her radio, she stood in our shop and began shouting louder and louder.

TOP SECRET: If a customer is having a blow out at your business location, ask them to step outside or to a separate space to discuss the issue. This will keep them from embarrassing you, themselves, and other customers.

As she exploded, I walked her outside and assured her we were addressing the issue.

"You've ruined my car" she exclaimed.

She then began cursing at me and anyone else within earshot. After asking her to please calm down several times I had to ask her to leave the premises. She refused and said she would call the police (example of why our tax dollars are so high). Long story short, it got uglier from there. The police came. She was told to leave because it was private property, I owned it. However, we still committed to making sure her car was operating properly if she would bring it back the next day so that we could take appropriate time to diagnose the problem. Her mother (a good customer) called and also complained.

The next day the young lady returned to our shop to have her radio repaired. My manager jumped into the car and pushed the "ON" knob. The radio played perfectly. It turns out that this customer kept her radio at full blast all the time. We turned it off during the service so that we could hear ourselves think.

She did not say anything but just jumped in her car and left. Her mother did call back and apologize which was appreciated. This agonizing experience taught me two things:

1. To be a better customer myself, particularly if I've had a bad day and am not living my best life that month. When I get bad service, I take deep breaths and repeat "Nobody died." That's my mantra.

2. Reminder, not everybody is your customer.

Whenever my employees call me and say "There is a problem with this customer, they have X type of car and we did X service." The first thing I ask is "What is their purchase history?"because I want to know whether that customer has spent a lot of money with my business. I'm not going to treat customers badly if it's their first visit, but I am going to bend over backward to keep my best customers happy the 80 – 20 rule. You make 80% of your $$$ from 20% of customers. This type of historical purchase information must be in your computer system, if not get a new computer system.

The good of customers? You will encounter numerous unassuming people who are truly wonderful and some truly in need. It has been my privilege to help many of them. For example, one Christmas Eve I loaned a woman my car to drive to her son's house over 500 miles away. Her car had overheated and was absolutely not drivable. I had other cars, she seemed nice, I'd never met her before but felt good about doing this, especially on Christmas Eve. Granted, she could have taken off and never returned, but I was in possession of her broken down car (that's called collateral) which had her license plate on it (I could trace that). She returned the following week, during which time we repaired her car, and was grateful and ecstatic.

I can't tell you how many customers I've served who forgot their wallets or their credit card wouldn't work or was declined. One young woman, who worked at the Panera Bread nearby, forgot her wallet. She was mortified, maybe thinking I might call the police or get upset. I told her to just go back to work and come back and pay us when she got off work. Her mouth dropped, she was speechless. I guess she could not believe that in this day and age you could come back later to pay, that anyone would trust you to come back. I was proud that we established that sense of trust and community with her and hoped she would tell her colleagues. Moreover, I knew where she worked. If she pulled a fast one, I could just go up to Panera and address the matter. She came back. She paid and we had a customer for life.

CONTRACTS

■ ■ ■

I always say, if you have to cheat your customer to make money, don't be in that business whatever it is. For example as a business owner, you will encounter vendors that want you to sign a contract. OK, fair enough (yes you do have to read the whole 3 page 6 font contract). Way down in the fine print the contract says that it automatically renews yearly if you do not notify them 60 days prior. This is typical for uniform companies, phone services, payroll and so on. I get that the company needs reasonable notice, but automatic renewal is bad business. This is something to keep that in mind if you are the one writing the contract for your customers to sign.

TOP SECRET: You can sign a multi page contract if you read it and simply strike through the things that you do not agree with or change the text like you might when you buy a house. Sign and return. *The vendor also never reads their contracts* and if you strike through that paragraph on page 4 mid way among dozens of other paragraphs, the one that says "automatic renewal", they won't see that until years later. Keep a copy.

IF YOU TOUCHED IT, YOU OWN IT

"99 percent of all failures come from people who have a habit of making excuses."

– George Washington Carver

■ ■ ■

There are times when you service something for a customer, perhaps you give them a haircut, do their nails or change their oil. During that process, things can go wrong. As you read in a prior chapter a customer can be in the wrong or unreasonable (broken radio story). However, if you cut someone's straight hair and suddenly it's falling out or you paint someone's nails and they all break off the next day or you change their oil and their oil light comes on (because the sensor is broken) you have to address the problem reasonably with the customer. I explain to my employees 'If we touch it, we own it'. That means that even though we probably didn't cause the problem, we need to address it.

What does it mean to address it? It could be anything from saying "I'm sorry that happened" (not I'm sorry we did that unless you did) to completely fixing the problem that you might *not* have caused at no charge to the customer. This is also called a "cost of doing business." Put yourself in your customers' shoes. If you encountered a seemingly related problem right after a service you would think the same. Doesn't mean you caused the problem but if you want to keep especially your good customers happy, you need to own the problem.

HR MANAGEMENT

■ ■ ■

All I can say it that you need this. Refer back to that chapter called "Employees the Good, the Bad, and the Ugly". While employees may seem eager when interviewing and motivated once working for you, if they leave most of them aren't happy. Whether they find another job or heaven forbid you have to fire them, they are not happy. You need to have your HR ducks in a row, CYA (cover your ass). You need to have done the proper basics, hiring forms, W4, I9, written employee handbook and so on. Needless to say, you need to be an upright, non prejudice, non harassing boss. This book assumes you are that as we discussed it in the early chapters.

As you know, I used to work in big corporate America and I knew that these HR requirements were real, I understood them loosely, but to be honest in my own business I sometimes let the day to day get in the way of doing them thoroughly. As a result, I've been bitten by the "are you kidding me?" bug a couple of times. And maybe I deserved it. So, I don't want you to do same. For example, when one employee resigned formally by letter, giving two-weeks notice etc… and then applied for unemployment payments (not valid in the state of Virginia). I had to go through a lot of paperwork and several phone calls with the unemployment commission for them to confirm to her that "No, you do not earn unemployment payments if you resign".

These are the basic HR filing requirements you must have:

1. I9-Federal form: for immigration (just shoot yourself, this is a nightmare).

2. W4 (payroll deductions): update these annually.

3. Employee Handbook: It will include things like: safety requirements, uniforms, smoking, attendance, on-the-job injury, absence reporting, payroll and so on. Yes, you have to have one. You truly will not believe what employees will or will not do unless it's in writing. "I forgot to tell you that I have to go pay my phone bill by 5pm and need to leave early." It's 4:45 pm. Sorry company policy states that we require 24 hours notice for early departure. A franchise will provide you with the employee handbook.

4. EEO Stuff : Read it. Become familiar, but don't let it run your company. Hire good people and be a good example. Dozens of companies will email or mail you to try and sell you expensive posters listing all the EEO and or OSHA requirements. Don't buy them! You get these posters for free from the appropriate state or local agency.

5. Performance write ups: A doc you can create yourself that documents unacceptable performance by an employee, for example multiple tardiness, lack of proper uniform, etc...Name, date, infraction have it signed by the employee and give them a copy.

TOP SECRET: Unscrupulous employees will file complaints against your business with state and local agencies like these because they are mad, you fired them legitimately or they quit out of anger.

This is not common but unfortunate. Sadly, you have to address the complaints whether they are valid or not. This can take a good bit of your time, is frustrating and means that you need to keep satisfactory documentation on employees always. **Bottom line, once you have things rolling in HR you might spend a couple of hours a month keeping this information up to date. Just do it!**

PAYROLL

■ ■ ■

It's important to have an automated system by which you pay your employees and to follow state and federal law closely. Don't be sloppy here. Once, I was sued by an employee on a payroll technicality. Let's be clear, I'm honest. I'm not looking for ways to cheat people and we operated honestly. She quit, legitimately and then reached out to a lawyer and complained about x,y,z,p,d,q. The lawyer said, none of those matter except Q (payroll). Tell me more. And from there filed a lawsuit.

OK, we are getting in the weeds here, but I lost the lawsuit, my lawyer said 'You are going to lose" and he was right. The total spend on this debacle was $40,000. $30,000 went to the lawyers and an average of about $110 each to employees. If you have a question in the payroll world, discuss it with your accountant or your processor. Make sure they put answers to you in writing (email).

If you have 10 or fewer employees you can probably do payroll yourself with input from managers. More employees than that you might hire assistance.

Some employees will tell you they don't have a bank account. Require them to have one. *You must pay by direct deposit, not check or other.* You will not survive the headaches. And 'yes" there are still lots of companies that still pay their employees by check, especially in businesses like mine. But yours won't. Cash cards that get reloaded by payroll systems are ok too.

Some employees, especially at lower-pay levels, may ask you for pay advances. *Just say no.* I wish I had. Early on, your employees will ask for pay advances to test your practices. If you bought the business from someone who allowed advances, you will need to stop that practice. If they did not allow advances, do not start this practice. It's very messy, hard to track, time consuming and unpleasant all the way around. With that said, I've given plenty employees pay advances. The majority of which I should not have, including the woman I bought a car for and she skipped town the following week. It's called learning. Now you know better.

THE DON'TS

"Can you just not."

– Taylor Swift, "You need to Calm Down," 2019

■ ■ ■

DON'T REINVENT THE WHEEL. Even if you are new to your business other people are not. Get on a forum, Meetup, business council and ask other successful business owners for their advice. Take that advice. If the advice seems wrong run it by another mentor. Have mentors. With that said, bring your personality to the table.

DON'T' GIVE TONS OF STUFF TO YOUR FRIENDS for FREE. You definitely can give your friends discounts.

> **TOP SECRET:** Add "VIP" to your friend's bill or to their names in your computer system so that staff knows that these people get a discount. But the service should not be FREE unless it's your mom. If you do give stuff to your friends, even small discounts, ask them for a review on social media. Send them a link. Make it easy and they will be happy to do so.

DON'T HIRE SPOUSES UNLESS THERE IS A REALLY GOOD REASON FOR IT. Not kidding.

DON'T CHEAT ON YOUR TAXES. You will ultimately cheat yourself. When you are ready to sell your business the sale amount will be based on your net income. That means, if you've cheated, by showing a lower net income, your business will sell for less.

DON'T STOP LEARNING. The more you learn, the more $$$ you will make.

DON'T MAKE EXCUSES. I find this to be very prevalent today. I will ask an employee in a business "Is there any more sugar for sale the type that was being sold for 1.99?" And they respond "Well" (You know what's next when they say "Well" the beginning of a lengthy stream of babble that you don't care about and don't want to hear).

"Well, Fred is on vacation this week and he usually orders the sugar. He musta' forgot to put that order in before he left and so the sugar didn't come in on the truck, at least that's what Sarah told me but she's not here today either. You could come back next week and see if Fred can help you."

As a business owner, the answer I would have preferred to hear was "No I'm sorry there is not but we do have this other brand it's great and it's $1.99 also." Do not lead your customer down this long and winding road, reinforce to your employees, our customers don't care about our problems here at the business. For example, who does what or who is on the schedule or not. Just help this customer. Solve their problem.

DON'T TALK ABOUT EMPLOYEES TO OTHER EMPLOYEES: 1. because you have better things to do that will make $$$ and 2. The information will get around the entire organization. It's going to come back to bite you. Tell your partner or bud instead.

YOU ONLY HAVE 1 JOB HIRE PEOPLE TO DO THE REST

You'll hear from friends, family and other business owners that as a business owner have to "do it all." That is and is not true. *You have to get it all done, but you don't have to do it all.* You have to make sure it gets done in a quality way, but you don't have to do it all, you have to make sure that what is getting done is adding value and that you are taking care of your customers, but you don't have to do it all. There are things you will outsource.

Reminder, as a business owner, you really have 1 job during years 1 to 3, and frankly beyond when you are working your 10 or 20 hours a week that is to connect with customers and build trust. My friend Victoria, the one that owns the dance studio, teaches people from ages 2 to 25. While she could focus on younger, middle or older students she's focused on the long term.

She told me, "I'm going to make sure I'm always on site for the teeny tiny kids aged 2 to 5 because that's when they develop a passion and a love for dance." It is so obvious, but not something I'd considered before. Her job is to connect.

As I mentioned, people want to do business with people they like and they need to like you. They don't need to love you; you don't need to be best friends; you need to connect. Ask about their dog, their car, their career. However, they can't decide if they like you if you are not in the shop because you have your head in the financials or your hands in a warehouse doing inventory. I've seen many people come from different backgrounds that cannot give up their prior career (accounting, HR, marketing and so on). The accountant that buys the bike rental shop but works at home on the books and never meets a customer, the banker that buys the salon and sees nothing but payroll, the IT guy/gal that buys an ice cream parlor and makes it so high tech, no one can figure it out. Your job as the business owner is to smile, shake hands and make sure your customers are happy, *getting value from your services.* Your job is sales.

Can you pay people to sell for you? Yes, but first you have to be able to do it yourself. You have to fully understand it. If there were a business where we could just do nothing and pay people to make us money we'd all be rich. That kind of business doesn't exist. You don't have to micro manage it or do it yourself forever but you do have to understand it.

Before you even buy your business, you will need both a lawyer and an accountant to help you set up your corporations. Because we have a huge job selling, we are going to outsource other things. Other than sales, the major responsibilities in any business include HR, Finance / Accounting, Marketing, and Operations. Hopefully you are good at one of these and you can contribute.

But as a business owner, you do need to understand what is going on in each of these areas. You need to have basic knowledge. If you have that, great, if not there are plenty of courses online or at the local community college (cc) that you can take to become knowledgeable. Do not ignore the local community college. I have a college degree yet have taken several courses at cc since I became a business owner. For me, it works better than online because it forces me to set aside time to educate myself on the subject and do my homework. As I mentioned, I've also had great experiences at Pryor.com and similar providers of 1 or 2 day sessions on accounting, marketing all of the above and more.

If you buy a franchise, they will typically recommend service providers for you in certain fields. If you buy an independent business, you will be barraged by people trying to sell you these services every day. Remember. COMPLEXITY = ENEMY. SIMPLICITY = SANITY. There will be a top two or three service providers locally or nationally, stick with them. You might consider using your barber's nephew or dog walker as your social media person but once they graduate from dog walking you'll be out of luck. Your neighbor is a bookkeeper, ok if they've done it for a long time, they are sane, savvy and stable and they aren't moving to Florida soon, you can use them.

You will pay for these services monthly. Never pay an upfront fee and be sure to negotiate. You have options. Ask for something free, an upgrade or an add-on. For example, if you purchase a Scheduling app ask them to throw in the Attendance upgrade for free. You got this. Don't sign a long term contract that's so 20th century.

For example, I'm good at IT and FINANCE. I do those things hands on for my businesses as a 2nd tier responsibility. That saves me $$ and allows me to keep my eyes on the prize (my money). But, I pay people to do my accounting, payroll, social media, repair building and equipment and sometimes help with hiring, preferably online.

OK. So you don't know a lot about IT, accounting or marketing you can learn enough to get rich realistically by hiring people to provide these services for you as long as you know enough to ask good questions. Here's some information on each of those, to start.

ACCOUNTING

"Life is like accounting, everything must be balanced."

– Unknown

■ ■ ■

Ask friends, mentors and industry people who to hire. You have to kiss some frogs before you will find your accounting prince or princess. The accountant typically provides your monthly cash flow statements and balance sheet and does your taxes. This person is very important to your business so make sure they are the right one for you and don't hesitate to fire them (move on gracefully) if they are not. The biggest issues with your accountant are typically communication and timeliness. If they do not return calls or emails that is not ok. If you do not get your financials quickly enough, that too is not ok.

TOP SECRET: Accountants sometimes have specialties for example they may do accounting for a lot of restaurants or for a lot of gyms. This may help you choose one that has more experience in your field, so ask.

TECHNOLOGY

■ ■ ■

Being tech savvy and knowing how to use technology in your business aren't exactly the same. You probably know how to download apps or process mobile payments, great! In your business, however, you need apps and systems that work together rather than being stand alone as they are in your personal life. There are three things to considering when managing your business systems. 1. You can't just swap them out in a hot minute like you can download an app because all your employees and customers have to be on board. 2. There is always going to be something better. Don't upgrade computers or systems until you measure (this means dollar and cents) the benefits. Your goal with your business IT is "good enough" because technology is not your biz, unless it is (i.e. you own a technology company.) Instead, your biz is a broken service company. 3. Never pay an IT company to build a custom application for you. Don't reinvent the wheel. Whatever you need it's already available somewhere.

Why not have a custom application built? What if the person who builds it wins the lottery? What if they die? What if they have a life crisis and disappear like one of my programmers did?

"They have a partner and there are other people in the company right?"

Maybe, but unless you are hiring a fairly large and costly IT firm, and keep the company on retainer you won't get upgrades or your software will break when a new version of Windows or iphone comes out. Whatever your business is there's an app for that.

Making changes to computer systems, apps, etc… no matter what someone tells you is going to be, is risky. Something is going to go wrong. Why? Programmers, much like the rest of us "are lazy." Years ago people used to test the heck out of computer systems. Now, especially if you are using an app that is free-ish, they don't test stuff, you do. The exceptions are payment and payroll processors, although I must say my payroll processor (big name co.) has had some serious outages. Like, how do you not pay your employees? That's not cool.

If you aren't tech savvy work on that. Take those community college classes (after year 1 of our plan). Technology is your friend and will allow you to watch your business' productivity and profitability while you're relaxing on the beach. Because by year 5, you will be cycling down to 20 hours a week and you will know your business financial stats and you will get them on your phone.

Backup your data. Just like at home, you can use Google or Apple or whatever but check on it monthly and make sure it's there. Your information and your customers information is everything.

Put virus protection on your computers. Duh. But I'm serious. I've heard of people losing everything or having their data stolen. If your company is sloppy someone can take all your data and hold it hostage. Is this is going to happen to you? Probably not. How long does it take each month to ensure that it does not, 15 minutes. Just do it.

If your computer system, smart phone, security system, internet or phone system are malfunctioning or go down unplug the device and wait a minute and then plug it back in. I know this may be obvious but if this happens and you are not present in the shop you'll need to advise your staff to do same. They will call you and act like they've never seen a modem before. If this simple solution doesn't work, call the company responsible (Verizon, Comcast etc…) and get them to fix it within 1 hour. As a business you pay for and require 100% up time on these services. If they say we'll have someone out in a week.

Scream at them until they come that day or next (assuming there is not a widespread outage).

MARKETING

"Good marketing makes the company look smart. Great Marketing makes the customers feel smart."

– Joe Chernov

■ ■ ■

I hate marketing. Why, because I'm a black and white person and marketing is gray, it's like purplish, blackish, yellowish. Google and other companies can provide metrics for clicks etc… Those are numbers, but they are hard for a small business to truly capture and act upon (read on). The most important thing to do with marketing is tie it directly to your customer base. Focus. Do not use the shotgun approach trying every type of advertising you've ever heard about sending it to all corners of the earth. You will waste so much of the money you need to get rich.

Sales people will come into your biz or call or email you daily to sell you a marketing product or service. Some services are real and great, some are a complete waste of money. If they won't give you a free trial that should tell you something. If they don't understand your business, don't hire them. They need to be able to tell you something about your customers that you don't know. If they do cool, you have my attention.

Let's assume your business is local because that's our goal. Local might be the bakery down the block or the paint company that covers the entire western side of the city, or you might build a service that is statewide (see chapter "My Business is Doing Great Should I Expand"). Nevertheless, focus. Identify your customers and think creatively about where they are and how to reach them cost effectively. Write down your customer profile on a white board or on your hand (never wash it off) and did I say this before, focus on them?

There are generally two types of marketing, specific service sales and general awareness (your brand). I can't tell you how many times people told me "I drive right by your business every day and I never knew what you did, you were there etc..." That's the awareness side of things. General awareness includes things like signage, uniforms, logos, tag lines and so on. Bottom line, *these are not DIY items.* My favorite source for logos, graphic design etc...is Fiverr.com where you will find great talent at great prices.

Specific product sales are driven by the marketing of that service. Focus on your most popular services, for example in the car biz it's all about the oil change, which people used to do four times a year. Now people change oil about twice a year, but that is still the most popular service for repair shops. Ads (see examples below) should focus on your most popular service, which might be seasonal recall the example of mountain biking tour in the summer and skiing in the winter or cooling in the summer and heating in the winter.

The best way to manage marketing is to develop a monthly marketing plan for a full year. Excel is a great tool for this because you can capture costs at the same time and ensure you are on budget. Keep in mind that some marketing efforts cost almost nothing. Attending your kids soccer game and handing out a few coupons is pretty much free, just the cost of the coupons. Double bonus, at the soccer game you get to smile and shake hands too. People will want to support you because you support their team. Posting about your business on Nextdoor or Facebook is almost free. It takes a little time, but not a lot of $$$.

I'm not a marketing expert; I'm a car repair expert. However, in the following sections I've captured the basics you need to know in case you too, are not a marketing expert.

Tag Line

"Just do it."

– Nike

What is a tag line, you ask? The most famous tag line of all time, in my opinion is Nike's *Just do it*. A tag line tells the story of your business in a short burst. Coming up with your business tag line can be fun and help you focus. It's fun because you really have to describe your whole biz in just a few words, to brainstorm perhaps with friends and to be able to cast aside bad ideas. For example if Nike's tag line were "Good for Lazy People" or "Better than Addidas." Neither of those is interesting, motivational or make you want to buy the product.

Currently, my businesses tag line is "Care free Car Care." The message is important because my customers are time constrained they don't want to deal with excuses, mistakes, administration and are willing to pay more for convenience. It's also good because of the alliteration (all c's in case you've forgotten from high school). I write this tag line on my print ads, my employee uniforms, coupons, and my hand so that even I don't forget. Now that I'm writing this, I'm going to write it on the bathroom mirror at work where my employees can see it because they need to adopt this slogan as well.

You'll note that I said "my current" tag line. You should freshen your tag line at least every two years. My last tag line was "Trust My Car Shop" (actual name not used) short, sweet, and speaks to the issue that lots of people have with trusting car repair shops.

If your service is not a fun one, your marketing message will likely be based on "safety" or "saving $$ long term", or peer pressure (others are doing this so you should too) everyone else is getting a colonoscopy you better as well. If your service is fun, your marketing message will just be pictures of people smiling and doing your thing. Lucky you.

Social Media, Blogging

Is a must, but hire someone unless this was your career. It really works best for businesses that are "fun" and "funny" and experiential. We love to see car wrecks, cat tricks and capers online. However, your dentist is not going viral on social media, neither are my car repair shops. You must have a presence on social media and can hire someone with a brain for about $100-150 bucks a month to do it for you. Keep posts short. Do not bore people. They don't want to know the benefits of a root canal they want to see videos of kitties playing with birds. Facebook and Instagram, are pretty much the basics (although I do not have Instagram for my shop), Instagram more so if your biz is visual (painting, dog walking, party planning). Today, Facebook is a must because it is the 800 lb gorilla. But I'll continue to update this list regularly so you can stay on top of things. Each one is right for certain businesses, but each one can also be a waste of time and money. Remember, as a business owner, you have to focus.

Twitter – I don't recommend Twitter unless your biz is news, content writing, events or you are a celebrity. Happy to debate.

Blog posts, yes. A study[6] found that content marketing (blogging) acquires *three times as many leads per dollar spent* in comparison to paid search (Google Ads). While the effectiveness of blogging isn't in question, for a new business, the costs might be. There are plenty of great tools out there that can help you build content for your business. Even Google for Business prompts you now for regular blog posts. Have pictures ready that relate to your topic. Again, Fiverr.com is my favorite go to for this source if you are not a great writer yourself.

---

[6] http://flip.it/ZVWHiO

Giveaways

I really like making donations to schools, charities and clubs where I know my customers will be. Make sure your customers *do* go to these places. If you are selling manicures the local men's book club probably won't work for you. Moreover, do not give "$500 Free Room Painting service" to a church way across town. If you have a passion for that church and want to give that church money do it, but that is not marketing for your local business. It's not reaching your customers.

As a business owner you will find that people ask you for donations frequently. If you've ever been in the PTA or worked for a nonprofit, you know why. Therefore, find your customers and do giveaways for events that your customers will attend. Donate your time and money to your other favorites outside of the business.

Like everyone, I screw up occasionally too. I've been doing a giveaway for a charity for a few years. It's a great cause for disabled children. When sending them my usual gift certificate for one year of free car care, I noticed their address is nowhere near my target audience. Got me! I still donate to their cause personally, because it's great but wrong of me to consider this as a "marketing" tool. It's not. *Focus.*

Word Of Mouth/Apps

Are truly the best and most affordable marketing tools. Join the local social club, civic organization or volunteer at an event with a pocket full of coupons; get on a board or PTA. You'll also want to make sure that info on websites like YELP and Google Biz where people write reviews is accurate. It's a good bit of work to maintain your information on the many national sites I'd recommend hiring a service to do it (again, not your dog walker). Most of us are familiar with the Nextdoor app, where you complain that someone forgot to pick up their dog poop in your neighborhood. This is a great place to learn about your customers and get word of mouth business recommendations, (especially if your service is dog walking). You can advertise on the site too. It doesn't get any more local than that. But be careful. People who spend their time complaining about their neighbors might not be your customers.

TOP SECRET: *You can actually manage getting fewer negative ratings on social media now.*

There are services that act as intermediaries. It's not that the customer cannot leave a negative rating; it's just that you as the business owner can see the rating before it gets posted. That gives you a chance to address and hopefully fix the problem first. With that said, *bad ratings make your business better. Fix the problem.*

Radio/Tv

I personally have not found radio or TV advertising to be useful in my businesses. I'm not saying I'm right, but the results are hard to measure. If you have multiple locations, particularly if they are geographically separated, I can definitely understand the benefit. If you have a franchise and they manage and recommend radio and TV, cool. However, if like some people, you just want to see yourself on TV and have people mention it to you, first, you should not be a business owner, second, work on your self-esteem. This is business not personal. When does TV work? Focus, find the programs that your customer watches, have a good message and solve your customers' problems. But yes, those things are true for all types of marketing.

Google Ads

I use Google Ads. As I said, I have a degree in technology. I can barely do the programming (yes programming) necessary to create my own ad campaign.

I just spent an hour on the phone with a Google employee who could not answer my questions about how the site worked. Google is working on it, but is not there yet. You can waste a lot of money on Google Ads and I have done that. I've tried outsourcing it too and still don't really know if I'm getting any bang for my bucks. *With that said, if the majority of your competitors are using Google Ads, you must too.*

Here's a Google Ads cheat sheet:

- Ads = what am I selling.
- Text in the ads = what is my competitive advantage Price? Best Product? Service? For example use words like "fast" "convenient" 'luxury model"

Make sure to narrow down the demographics setting to target only your customers (you can do this by gender, age, zip code etc...) or you'll waste a lot of money on clicks from people in Australia.

Give Away Something For Free

I learned this from a marketing friend and it helped me a lot. If you are able, and I can't really imagine a business that cannot, give away something for free, even if it is with a purchase. Obviously you *give away something that costs you very little in comparison to what you are selling.* For example a dog walking service (little bucks) might offer a free dog wash for first- time customers. A moving company (big bucks) might offer five free boxes for your move. In my car repair business I give away free towing to my shop up to 5 miles (cap my loss). This costs me about $45 because I have negotiated a good rate with the towing company. When the car arrives we diagnose and repair it for a minimum value of about $100 but perhaps $1000 or more. We are an honest and competent shop so we find that typically these people have a good experience return and become regular customers. Why? I'm solving two big problems for them – towing and repair. Do I lose money, sometimes? Do I make money the majority of the time? Yes. People love getting something for free.

TOP SECRET: Don't just give something away for free and say goodbye, put the cost of the free service on the invoice and then deduct it as a discount. That way, the customer will be reminded of the benefit even months later.

Don't we all think "Well, I was at the barber shop today and they gave me a free hot towel treatment" Or

"I was at the nail salon today and they gave me a free nail file!"

Word of mouth!

Cross Promotion

Is when you work with one or more businesses with which you share customers. For example, a child's clothing store partners with a theme park or a car repair shop with a car wash; those work. A maternity shop and a skateboarding store? Um no. It's very much like referrals and can work formally or informally. The answer as always is to focus on who your customer is and create relations with businesses who can refer those customers to you. A chimney sweep (does anyone even know what this is anymore?) and a gas log installer. Yes!

With this type of marketing both businesses win and typically the costs are low. At the same time, you might meet another business owner who can become a friend, colleague, mentor, and advisor or vice versa.

To summarize, in my opinion marketing is most challenging because its results are hard to quantify. If you are good at marketing that will be a plus as an entrepreneur, if not, always remember:

- Who your customer is,

- Where you can find them,

- To Focus – pick three or four marketing initiatives, maybe two branding and two specific ads and run those for three to six months. You are not going to know if they are working sooner. Measure – keep track of ads and coupons coming in,

- To outsource marketing unless you are a guru,

- To develop an monthly marketing calendar with a specific budget.

LEGAL STUFF

"Laws control the lesser man...Right conduct controls the greater one".

– Mark Twain

■ ■ ■

In your small business the majority of legal advice you will need will concern, business organization (setting up a corporation or two) human resources (chapter "HR"), taxes, licenses and fees. For most of these issues, you might consider services like LegalZoom.com or similar. They do an adequate job for these purposes. However, LegalZoom and others are mostly automated making the process kind of like filling out your taxes, there will be terms that you don't understand, and if you check the wrong box you might be in trouble. Better yet ask sane, savvy, stable friends and family or your accountant for a referral for a business attorney.

THE END: YEARS 8 THROUGH 10

Yes! We've made it to the final phase. During years 8 through 10 we will be doing a few key things:

1. Continuously improving our business and sales.

2. Perhaps buying our property if we have not already.

3. Preparing to sell our business.

4. Saving $$$ because we are making lots.

5. Developing our lead employees and manager(s).

MY BUSINESS IS DOING GREAT SHOULD I EXPAND

■ ■ ■

The answer to this question is in the first five words, "My business is doing great." So, there are three considerations,

1. Are you making 6 figures a year as we planned?

2. Are you working the hours we predicted (20 hours per week years 3-7, 10 hours week years 8-10)

3. Is your business operating like a top, all the biz you can do at this location and you are in the top 10% compared to peers?

I just threw that last point in there as a challenge. Last, on top of all that, what does your family think?

If you are succeeding and have bandwidth (free time), then yes, consider expanding. If the answer is no, review your plan and have a mentor review your biz to find out why not. For example, let's say you own a catering business and it's netting you $50k a year. Nice, but that's not our goal. Our goal is $100K plus. So, you have to evaluate whether this shop can produce more or a 2nd location or expansion is needed to reach our goal. I would recommend that 2nd location be your 2nd choice not your first choice. Extract as much profit as you can from location 1 before you consider location #2. Perhaps you can extend your business hours or be open on weekends. Perhaps you can add online services. Either of those should happen before you add a 2nd location, only because a 2nd location is hard. If you are not making $$ hand over fist, the answer is no, do not expand to do so. That's like re-using a dirty diaper. If it isn't' clean don't put it on your other kid. If your first kid is potty trained can say "Mom" and "Dad" and is starting to dress themselves then OK it might be time to have another one.

When considering a second location or diversifying your business horizontally or vertically (email me about this one.) You have to have a solid foundation of financials, employees, processes and slack (free time, real free time). Most importantly, you must have good-great manager in biz #1 that can allow you to focus on biz #2.

If you are a franchise, the franchisor will help you identify a second location. But beware. They like to have as many locations as possible. If you go broke it's on you not them.

So, let's say you do have a great biz going and you have slack. The other thing I want you to consider is lifestyle. Are you making great money now, do you have the family time we planned for? Do you have the support from your family or franchise to open another business and go back to years 1-3 where you may have to work 50 to 80 hours a week for a while to get that thing up and running? True, it's likely that it won't be as hard as the first one, but it will be a load. What is enough?

If you are like me, there is never enough (meditation helps). I've opened 4.5 auto repair shops. The .5 was a car wash that I developed, but chose not to build. I closed one shop that wasn't performing well and I've sold two. I'm down to 1 business; I work 10-15 hours a week, meet my financial goals and am very happy about that. I've purchased my properties (and will tell you how later) and I'm excited for what is next. So, just take a moment, take a breath and say, "Do I have it in me and my family to expand my business?" If the answer is yes, cool. You know the drill. If the answer is "no," that is the right. You do you. *There is no shame in being simply successful.*

LOCATION, LOCATION, LOCATION

■ ■ ■

You've heard this before; real estate is all about location, location, location. If your business is drive by or walk by (that means customers come to you) then the location is critical and long term if you can purchase this real estate you will hit the jack pot. Even if you go to your customers' locations then your goal is to be more central or have access to highways to get you to your customers quickly. Buying either of them will be a plus.

If your location caters to foot traffic or drive in, it needs to be a great location as evidenced by foot traffic numbers you can find online or from realtors. The location is even better if it is close to your home, is a place you can walk to or drive to in less than 30 minutes. Remember if you aren't there, you can't shake hands.

If you are going to purchase your location here are some of the challenges:

- Confirm the walking or driving traffic count. (This is akin to 'run the numbers' that you did before buying your business). Do this early and often.

- Environmental: If you are in any kind of business that requires hazardous materials, such as plumbing, auto, electrical, cleaning, salon almost anything you may be required to do environmental testing of your site before you can get a loan to buy it. These tests are called Phase 1 and Phase 2. They cost thousands of dollars each so you'll need to incorporate that into your real estate purchase budget.

- Neighbors, competition. Declining or increasing?

- Commercial appraisal of a property is $5000 and up.

- Conventional bank loans require 20% down payment while an SBA (small business association) bank loan typically requires 10% down.

- Codes, building specs, signage. There are city, state and local codes for many parts of your business. If you are buying an empty shell you'll have a lot to learn about them. To remove those hurdles, *I recommend buying a building that is already operating (just as you bought an existing business) as you will operate it if possible.* Review your local business requirements.

Buy your real estate if you can. Control your own destiny.

HOW TO BUY THE REAL ESTATE

"Success = when the street is closed and you find a short cut."

– Champe

■ ■ ■

We are going to assume that you have rented your location. However, buying it is a big deal, the goal, the icing on the cake. If you already own your location, then you are in a great position. If not, doing so is a way to solidify your exit from the business in year 10 or whenever you are ready rather than allow the landlord to hold all the cards when your lease is up.

As you move through years 5 through 7 operating your biz you better be saving some $$$ because that's what we have to do, to GRR. There are several good options for your savings like paying off any loans you had on the biz to remove debt, expanding your biz, or investing in your biz to make even more money. But you are financially savvy or you would not be here. Paying off debt is always a plus, saving too.

However, what I'm recommending is that eventually, you do buy the location in which you operate your business. Save a down payment to position yourself in these good years to buy the commercial real estate on which you operate. It may be a warehouse for $100,000 or it may be a $1,000,000 site with the potential for top dollar development.

I realize that not everyone is going to be able to buy the real estate. I get that. For example, I cannot imagine the rent paid by a car repair shop in San Francisco or NYC. But most of us don't live there. We live Other City, USA. Moreover, putting your kids through college may be a bigger priority for you. Legitimate. But, if you follow this plan, you will be positioned to buy the real estate you are renting and there are several ways to do it.

First, decide if you want to buy your real estate? Is the location right for you and the biz? Is the area improving or declining? Has it been successful? Have you been able to achieve your financial and lifestyle goals in that location? Do you have the space you need to grow, add new services, store inventory, house employees? If the answer is "yes" then go for it. If the answer is "no" that's OK too because maybe there is a better, cheaper location that you can buy. Either way, there are several options very much like the options you had to buy your biz. However, good news you've now established yourself as an "owner operator" you've saved a down payment and hallelujah, *banks will actually, lend you money.* I'm not saying it will be easy, but they will.

TOP SECRET: However, my secret to success in real estate has been to buy the property from the owner using owner financing.

Once you know that you want to own the property, our goal would be to get the current owner to finance the purchase for several reasons. 1. Getting a bank loan for commercial property is hard, 3 times as hard as refinancing a home 2. You can control the terms of the loan by negotiating with the owner whereas, a bank sets the terms for you 3. Depending on the process the loan may not show up on your credit report / debt schedule as it is a private loan.

Begin the owner financing discussion in years 5 to 7. By that time, you've proven that the business is successful and you are meeting the goals we've defined in our 10 year plan. Start thinking about the real estate purchase *from the owner's perspective.* Are they ready for retirement, had a major life change or maybe live far away? Throw it out there to them "If you ever want to sell the property, let me know" once or twice a year because this process can be very good for the owner too.

Let's say that the owner is interested in selling the property to you and you've saved what you know to be the appropriate down payment, (a private owner might accept a 5 or 10% down payment whereas a bank will require 20 to 25%) ask them for a meeting to discuss. Prior to the meeting *you must have comps* for the property and do your homework finding out what they paid for the building originally and what similar properties are selling for now (comps). And obviously, know what you can afford as a down payment.

Meet with the owner and let them do all the talking; listen, find out what's going on in their world. Do they need cash because they want to buy a condo in Florida? Do they want long-term cash flow for retirement? Perhaps they thought their son-in-law was going to take over the business and now he's not. Listen. It's challenging, but important. You will need to find out what they want so that you can craft an offer for the owner to match their needs, just like you've done all this time for your customers. Solve their problems.

If the building owner is open to selling and has given you a purchase price, counter lower just as you would when buying a house. Your offer can be via email, simple, not formal unless you are communicating through a real estate company or lawyer and it will include these basic terms: I will put xx % down, at xx% interest rate with a xx year amortization" usually 20 years and close in x months. The more expensive the property the farther out the closing typically because you will want to do 'due diligence". A purchase contract (written by a real estate lawyer) will follow and can recommend the right steps toward due diligence. To be honest, unless you are buying a property that costs a million or above, people actually still talk to each other during negotiations and shake hands. Eventually all the agreements go in a long messy contract.

If you signed a good lease originally, you don't need this deal. You don't need any deal. If you *need* the deal, you'll get a bad deal. When I bought my 3rd property, I had offered the owners a deal three times before and each time they said no. One time I said no to them when they countered and we ended negotiations. That is also ok. A deal gets done when it's right for both parties at the right place and the right time. Don't be desperate for any deal. There are a million more out there. Be patient. And try not to tell friends and family your plans until an agreement is signed because once you tell people then you feel obligated to proceed. You can always say "We might buy the property, but it has to be at the right price." And that is true. If it's too expensive you have to let it go. That might be hard because you feel invested, but this is business not personal. It's kind of like speeding. Yeah, I was speeding and I got a ticket for $100 or I could have left my home 10 minutes early and not gotten a ticket. In hindsight we wish we'd left early. Be patient. We are talking about big bucks here tens or hundreds of thousands of dollars. Know that this process will take months, possibly more than a year. Meanwhile, you can also consider moving the biz or buying a similar location. Read on, you have options.

CAN I GET RICH AND NOT OWN MY REAL ESTATE

■ ■ ■

Yes! But, you must have at least a 10-year lease (can be in two five year leases or similar) in place in order to sell your business wherever it is located. This is how it works. You'll run the biz for 10 years, working super hard years 1-3, working 20 hours a week years 4 through 7 and working 10 hours a week years 8 through10 making six figures annually, saving money and paying off debt (investing in yourself). When you are ready to sell, the person you sell your business to will pay you a lump sum or monthly payments. They too will likely run the business for ten plus years after which they can sell. We'll talk more about this cycle in the Exit Strategy chapter, how to sell, who to sell to and how to get your $$$.

If you do not buy the location you rent or you can move. Cities change. Bad neighborhoods become good and vice versa. You are not stuck. Consider moving or consolidating your businesses or merging with someone who does something similar to you. Learning and thinking about the future is a must. Every year think about your location, the real estate, and where you are going, literally.

EXIT STRATEGY YEAR 10 (LEAVE WITH A POCKETFUL OF $$$)

> "How lucky I am to have something that makes saying goodbye so hard."
>
> **– A.A.Milne, "Winnie the Pooh."**

Won't times change; businesses be eliminated, robots take over the world? Yes, yes, and not completely. Remember, as you've run your business successfully the last 10 years the same things were happening. Times were changing and you changed with them. I ran a quick lube for years that focused exclusively on oil changes. As I mentioned, people used to change the oil in their car four times a year, now it's about one to two times. To continue to be successful, I changed the business, I offered new services, I stayed abreast of the industry direction and I understood where it was going. You will too.

Woot, woot! Congrats! You've worked your way through decision making, deciding whether you'd be a good business person, you've heard the good; the bad and the ugly about entrepreneurship, employees and customers and you have a reference for tackling some of the deep dark secrets of business operation that no one else will tell you. High five! And now, here we are at the end, the exit strategy. You may or may not know what an "exit strategy" is. Simply put, it's how to sell your business. But you aren't just trying to get out of your business.

TOP SECRET: I'm going to tell you how to get out *when you want to, have a buyer lined up and get you the best sale price.*

Your exit is going to be either: years 8 through 10 (depending on your goals) or whenever the heck you want after that. Maybe, like me, you dig what you are doing, you are working 10 hours a week, you are making 6 figures and you want to keep going. You see the future for your biz, it's well-positioned, there are barriers to entry and you have a good reputation. However, if you want to sell, here's what you need to do.

In years 8 through 10, if you've followed the plan and have managed your finances appropriately, you'll be ready to start thinking about selling. First thing you might ask is "What is my business worth?" Good news. There are online stats that can give you this answer for almost any industry. You have to look at them early and often. Typically the number is a *multiple (times 3 or 5 is common) of your net income or 1 x your gross income.*

If your net income is $100,000 plus, which is our goal then your sales price should be 3 -5 x $100,000 or $300-500k but, it gets better. When you define your net income, you get to add back your personal and discretionary expenses and salary. For example, most people charge their cell phones to the company. So, add back $100 per month to your net income. Or perhaps you go to a franchise meeting in Hawaii each year that costs $3000. Add that back into profit too. Top that off with a $40,000 a year salary (ask your accountant to set this number for you early on) by the time you add these back into the net income, that net income might be $150,000. Much more than we started with, resulting in a sale price of 3-5 x $150,000. Now, you are selling for $425k or more. Congrats. And, that is not including the real estate profits if you own that.

In summary, your business is worth:

NET INCOME + DISCRETIONARY EXPENSES and
SALARY x 3 OR 4 OR 5 ish.

"Hey, there is a big difference between times 3 and times 5!"

You are right. That difference, as we said in the beginning, like everything else, is negotiable. Just as you might price your home or car above market to sell, start out on the higher end, giving yourself room to negotiate. If you own your real estate or can offer a long term lease to the buyer the price might be higher. Perhaps you are in a great location and Starbucks just moved in next door. Ka-Ching! More monies. Or, let's say you own an auto repair shop that is not open on Saturday. The buyer could open on Saturday and perhaps net an extra $20-30k a year. Tell them that in the negotiations because it's a great reason for them to pay more. Always think about what the buyer wants during your negotiation just like we do with our customers. What's in it for them? Solve their problems.

HOW TO FIND YOUR BUYER

■ ■ ■

Now we know what our business is worth. *How do you find someone to buy it?* Do you hire a business broker? Do you complain that no one will buy our business or that it's hard to sell a business? No! You create your own buyer. The *best way to sell your business* is to sell it to your employee, friend, customer, vendor, or other known person. We are going to position you and that buyer for the deal. Here's how.

First, of course, the person must have an interest in business owner-ship and the personality to succeed, as you did. Perhaps you have a partner in the business or a trusted manager, start talking to them in year 8 and on, to find out if they might be interested in buying the business. No pressure, just conversation.

Perhaps you have a customer that thinks your service is great or you have a vendor that you do a lot of business with or an employee of that vendor or even a great employee of a competitor? Dig, do your homework, think. It could be your child, your brother or sister in law or a neighbor, but they have to pass the same tests you did:

- Are they interested in owning the business?

- Are they sane, stable, financially savvy and have savings?

- Do they have access to some money and good credit?

- Do they own a home?

If the answer is yes to all of these questions then get that conversation started. And, there may be more than one person who would be right to buy your biz. *Talk to multiple potential buyers* over the years. It's like dating. Some are going to work out and some not. This process will take 1 to 3 years. Keep that conversation going and weed out the duds. Set goals. By year 10 you need to start doing the deal which means:

- Having two or more buyer candidates.

- Crafting a Letter of Intent and thinking about the terms of the sale.

- Defining how much on-going support you will provide them.

- Getting lawyers involved. (Especially define what happens if the deal goes badly.)

If you think your sister in law is the right person (she's passed requirements 1 to 4 above) but in year 9 (your schedule) she moves to Tibet to become a Buddhist priestess that won't work. You have to cut her loose and you need to have other candidates in the wings. People grow, change their minds, buy other businesses, get scared, whatever. You need to have several good candidates during these years.

So these candidates are interested in owning their own business. And they have the personality. Can they afford to buy it? Refer back to the chapter called "How Do I Afford to Buy the Business." Many of the same principles will apply for them. They could get loans from friends and family, use home equity, 401K or retirement. As I said before, I really don't like people getting loans from friends and family unless I believe in the success of the buyer. Honesty is the best policy. If you know you have a good business and the buyer is capable, and the friends or family have money that is not their last dime, then I would recommend this approach. If you believe the buyer is going to fail don't go there. Find another buyer. There are plenty of fish in the sea. If you've done this right, you will have multiple qualified buyers. You don't want the buyer to fail.

Technically the best exit is to find a buyer who has a down payment and can get a loan from a bank for the remainder. This allows you to walk away clean with your $$$. A bank *will* lend money to someone *experienced in the business that has good credit and a down payment.*

However, if the buyer has a down payment or home equity and good credit, you could also consider holding a note (loan) from them in order for them to buy the business. The benefits here are several. First, you know the person. Second, you know the business. You don't want to have to come back and clean up a mess but if you had to you could. Third you will get not only your sale price but interest on the loan you are holding for them that is a very nice benefit for retirement and some tax benefits. The buyer might get a home equity loan/line to pay you 20% down and you will float a note for 80%. Let's do the math.

Let's say my business is worth $300,000. My manager is a good operator and owns her own home. She can get a home equity line or family loan for $60,000 leaving a $240,000 debt. First option we all prefer is that this person gets a bank loan and we walk away whole. Many SBA loans are very doable for long term businesses if the buyer has good credit and experience. Second, a conventional bank loan for your manager (good luck.) Perhaps lightening will strike and the buyer will be able to arrange this. If neither of these works, fear not. You are still in luck.

You as the seller will hold that debt (get a lawyer involved to button this up and do a UCC Uniform Commercial Code filing) define the terms (monthly payments, timeframe and interest rate, closing date) that will provide you with the $$$ you need to do whatever you have planned next meanwhile "leaving meat on the bone" for the buyer. "Leaving meat on the bone" means that this sale has to be a win-win. You don't want the payments to be so high that the buyer goes out of business. Perhaps you have to take a longer loan term, 10 years instead of 5 but you get a higher interest rate? Sell your business allowing it to be profitable for the next person but never at your own loss.

When you sell, put clauses in the contract stating that the buyer must provide you with financials yearly. That way you'll know whether or not they are going to survive long term. Specifically, are they going to be able to pay back the money you lent them? If they are not, you have to be prepared to step back in or resell the business. Returning is not the goal but, it may be OK because you've had a few years off and you may be ready for a 2nd round. Moreover, you've been paid by the buyer for a period of time. Again, not our goal, but we are still in a good place because you get to keep the money paid to you to date. In fact, I am in this position now, not taking back, but carefully monitoring to see how my buyer is doing. I read their web reviews, drive by the business and ask friends. It doesn't take a lot of times, but it can help prevent unpleasant surprises.

Hundreds of thousands for the sale of your business, plus the money you've saved over the years = rich in no uncertain terms. Maybe you own your real estate and collect rent too. You definitely have enough to live off and retire to Mexico. If it's not enough, don't sell yet or do sell and find another stream of income. Perhaps your partner will continue working, or you'll start teaching yoga and make some money or do the Uber thing. This book is not about whether you are ready to retire; it's to help you get rich and create a great lifestyle by buying, running and selling your successful business when you are ready.

Just so you know, a smooth business sale will take 3-4 months. A bumpy sale (I've had a couple) will take 6 months to a year or die. During the negotiation you are still working hard at your biz. You are still looking for backup buyers. Do not take off for the Bahamas, this sale could fall through! The person you are selling to might have thousands in credit card debt, a bad credit score, the family won't lend them money or whatever. No matter what, it isn't sold until the $$ are in the bank. Celebrate at the closing! And most importantly, keep your mouth shut. Don't tell anyone about the sale until closing and *have the buyer sign a non disclosure* as part of the purchase agreement that says they won't discuss anything until the deal is done.

If this deal falls through, circle back to your next buyer. Keep on making six figures and getting rich realistically. Learn new things to stay motivated. Set new goals (3 each day, week, month and year). Keep your business and your books clean, and your staff motivated. If you've made it this far successfully, you know that. You wouldn't be here unless you understood. If it were easy, everyone would do it. I will also say that I ran one of my businesses for 15 years and when I sold, many of my customers were very near and dear to my heart. I wonder about some of them that I haven't seen, I learned from them, I saw their kids grow up. It's nice. You want someone good to continue in your customers lives.

WHAT I LEARNED AND LOVED

"Your work is going to fill a large part
of your life, and the only way to be truly
satisfied is to do what you believe is great
work. And the only way to do great work
is to love what you do."

– Steve Jobs, Chairman and CEO, Apple

■ ■ ■

That was awesome. I, me, myself found this great service business that was a "broken business". I bought it (and maybe a couple like it) and tweaked them to become profitable making me over $100k a year each. I worked double-time the first 3 years. In fact, I worked 6 days a week year 1 without a single day off. I nurtured my businesses during years 4 through 7 reaching out, meeting my customers, laughing and shaking hands, fine tuning and always improving staff.

Meanwhile, I was also looking for that potential employee that might purchase the business from me when I was ready. Many employees were not the right person, but I kept my eyes on the ones that were hard working, ambitious, had a great support system and maybe even better connections than I did. I gave that person my attention, educated them and helped them be ready to become owners, to buy the businesses that I loved, to pay me a premium for my 10 years of effort while leaving them a very profitable long term gig. This is the successful business cycle.

I didn't win the lottery, technically. I didn't inherit millions and I didn't invent a viral app. I just followed this plan.

I'm grateful, fortunate, curious and looking forward to what is next. Perhaps another business that is more of a hobby, perhaps becoming a full-time mentor (and by full time I mean 10 hours a week) perhaps moving to Spain, going back to school or teaching math who knows? But I am free to do that now because I've followed this plan time and again.

Life is very different working in corporate America vs. owning your own business. You don't just control your own destiny; you control the destiny of others. And you can do that in a good way or in a bad way. Whenever I felt bad about myself for some reason or other, my mother would say, "You know Champe, you are employing 10 (20, 30) people. They go home at night and take care of their families, they pay their rent, and they feed their children because of you." I didn't realize that as much early on, but after these years, and particularly since she died, I do. You remember that person you worked for when you were 20 or 30 years old who you still think about? They helped you, they loaned you money or they taught you something you'll never forget. I want that to be me. I want that to be you.

I've taught employees how to dress at work; how to speak to customers; how to eat properly and how to look people in the eye and shake their hands, all things that are important in business and that make you successful. I've been to the homes of my employee to help them move, I've babysat their kids so they could work, and I've given them clothes and furniture, and sadly sometimes I had to buy them food. I hope to be that person who teaches my employees and guides them and prepares them for their next gig that will be bigger and better than their current one and have told so many employees "I don't care if you work here or in the White House, you have to tuck your shirt tail in!" OK, that may be outdated but you get the idea.

I tell them that I want them to leave my employee to go some place more challenging. I give them training and yes sometimes I correct their grammar like Mom. I've helped at least one person buy their own business, changing the course of his family's life. That person has gone from being a GED laborer to a business owner. That success is something of which I'm most proud and I hope to do that for others.

I grew up in a family that valued education and knew I'd be going to a good college. Many of my friends have become doctors, engineers and lawyers. They make the big bucks. Right? $250, $300, $500 an hour? The problem is they still have to work a lot of hours and I don't. At least not much more than 10 hours a week. Am I smarter than them no? But what I have always known is how I did and did not want my lifestyle to be. I don't want to get up at 6am every day and rush into the office no matter how fancy that office is. I've taken risks to do what I do and some times I've failed. Most of the time, I succeed. And now although their parents get to say "Little Martha has become partner at XYZ law firm," I get to go fishing or to a concert with my niece on a weekday" and Martha has to work till midnight to sue people.

As a business owner, you will have the ability to do the same. You have the ability to build wealth for your family, to be creative, to solve problems, to dream, to touch your customers and community in amazing ways. Whether you give a job to a handicapped person, or donate services to someone in need or just keep your business looking great so that the neighborhood makes people smile, you can have an extraordinary impact. Meanwhile, *get rich realistically.* Start now.

I'M HERE TO HELP

So, you've read this book, you get it and you want to own and run your own business. Of course you do. You thought that before you bought the book. And now you know you can do this successfully. You've evaluated yourself. You've looked in the mirror and have been realistic. You've read the good, the bad, the hard and the easy wait, there isn't an easy. But there is fun and there are rewards and there is success. I'm with you I will continue to update this book so you can have the most current insights and references.

Way back when, I truly didn't know how to run a business although I thought I did. I had and education, possessed common sense and I had a bit of savings. But now I know that I could have done this early in life if I'd read this book. The key issues are to identify the right business, pay the right price, operate it properly and sell it for big bucks. I've done it time and again and you can too.

You got this and I'm here to help. Let's get it started, let's identify your business, and make this happen together. Email me, let's chat. Like a counselor or psychologist, I'm here to help you succeed through the process of buying, operating and selling a business just as I did.

You can buy a business; you can run it and you can GET RICH REALISTICALLY.

Champe@GetRichRealistically.com

BIZ TERMS

TERM	DEFINITION
CASH COW	You're making a lot of money. High five!
DUAL CONTROL	Never put $$ in the hands of any one person other than yourself. If one person counts the money, someone else must deposit it. Or if one person deposits it, someone else must check the bank statement for that deposit.
BARRIER TO ENTRY	This does not mean that something is making it hard to find your business location; instead, it's the stuff that makes it hard for people to copy your business. For example, in the car repair world we have expensive car lifts. If you start a rock climbing business you will need a great location and equipment. Both businesses are services and somewhat expensive making it difficult for just anyone to enter. Something that is hard to achieve like a 'master electrician" certification or legal degree is also considered a barrier.

PIVOT	Change direction. This word is used primarily by startups, mostly IT, when their idea is failing. Used in a sentence: "George, dude, we've spent $250,000 of our parents money on our "Find Best local Bourbon app" and it's going nowhere. I think we should pivot maybe re-write the app for GIN."
TERMS	"Of a contract" Down payment, timeframe, payments and interest related to a loan. For example, I'm going to buy this car for $500 down and $350/mo. For 5 years. Other issues may also be addressed here, but these are primary.
LOI	Letter of Intent. Can be found on line or from your attorney indicating that you want to buy something from someone or they want to buy something from you. State general terms but not all details.
EIN	Employer Identification Number EIN – Federal Tax ID: It's a social security number for your business. Your accountant can help or get it here: https://sa.www4.irs.gov/modiein/individual/index.jsp It's free!